Collins English Readers

Amazing Leaders

Level 4
CEF B2

OLDHAM COLLEGE

BARCODE.... CT0S663

CLASS No..... ER MES

DATE..... Jan 2015

D1585939

Text by
Katerina Mestheneou

Series edited by
Fiona MacKenzie

Collins

HarperCollins Publishers
77–85 Fulham Palace Road
Hammersmith London W6 8JB

10 9 8 7 6 5 4 3 2 1

Original text
© The Amazing People Club Ltd

Adapted text
© HarperCollins Publishers Ltd 2014

ISBN: 978-0-00-754507-0

Collins® is a registered trademark of
HarperCollins Publishers Limited

www.collinselt.com

A catalogue record for this book is available
from the British Library

Printed in the UK by Martins the Printers

All rights reserved. No part of this book
may be reproduced, stored in a retrieval
system, or transmitted in any form or
by any means, electronic, mechanical,
photocopying, recording or otherwise,
without the prior permission in writing
of the Publisher. This book is sold subject
to the conditions that it shall not, by way
of trade or otherwise, be lent, re-sold,
hired out or otherwise circulated without
the Publisher's prior consent in any form
of binding or cover other than that in
which it is published and without a similar
condition including this condition being
imposed on the subsequent purchaser.

HarperCollins does not warrant that
www.collinselt.com or any other website
mentioned in this title will be provided
uninterrupted, that any website will be
error free, that defects will be corrected, or
that the website or the server that makes it
available are free of viruses or bugs. For full
terms and conditions please refer to the site
terms provided on the website.

These readers are based on original texts
(BioViews®) published by The Amazing
People Club group.® BioViews® and The
Amazing People Club® are registered
trademarks and represent the views of the
author.

BioViews® are scripted virtual interview
based on research about a person's life and
times. As in any story, the words are only
an interpretation of what the individuals
mentioned in the BioViews® could have
said. Although the interpretations are
based on available research, they do not
purport to represent the actual views of
the people mentioned. The interpretations
are made in good faith, recognizing that
other interpretations could also be made.
The author and publisher disclaim any
responsibility from any action that readers
take regarding the BioViews® for educational
or other purposes. Any use of the BioViews®
materials is the sole responsibility of the
reader and should be supported by their own
independent research.

Cover image © Ruslan Grumble/
Shutterstock

MIX
Paper from
responsible sources

FSC
www.fsc.org
FSC™ C007454

FSC™ is a non-profit international organisation established to promote the
responsible management of the world's forests. Products carrying the FSC
label are independently certified to assure consumers that they come from
forests that are managed to meet the social, economic and ecological needs
of present and future generations, and other controlled sources.

Find out more about HarperCollins and the environment at
www.harpercollins.co.uk/green

✦ CONTENTS ✦

OLDHAM COLLEGE

BARCODE...

CLASS No...

DATE...

◆ INTRODUCTION ◆

Collins Amazing People Readers are collections of short stories. Each book presents the life story of five or six people whose lives and achievements have made a difference to our world today. The stories are carefully graded to ensure that you, the reader, will both enjoy and benefit from your reading experience.

You can choose to enjoy the book from start to finish or to dip into your favourite story straight away. Each story is entirely independent.

After every story a short timeline brings together the most important events in each person's life into one short report. The timeline is a useful tool for revision purposes.

Words which are above the required reading level are underlined the first time they appear in each story. All underlined words are defined in the glossary at the back of the book. Levels 1 and 2 take their definitions from the *Collins COBUILD Essential English Dictionary* and levels 3 and 4 from the *Collins COBUILD Advanced English Dictionary*.

To support both teachers and learners, additional materials are available online at www.collinselt.com/readers.

The Amazing People Club®

Collins Amazing People Readers are adaptations of original texts published by The Amazing People Club. The Amazing People Club is an educational publishing house. It was founded in 2006 by educational psychologist and management leader Dr Charles Margerison and publishes books, eBooks, audio books, iBooks and video content, which bring readers 'face to face' with many of the world's most inspiring and influential characters from the fields of art, science, music, politics, medicine and business.

◆ The Grading Scheme ◆

The Collins COBUILD Grading Scheme has been created using the most up-to-date language usage information available today. Each level is guided by a brand new comprehensive grammar and vocabulary framework, ensuring that the series will perfectly match readers' abilities.

		CEF band	Pages	Word count	Headwords
Level 1	elementary	A2	64	5,000–8,000	approx. 700
Level 2	pre-intermediate	A2–B1	80	8,000–11,000	approx. 900
Level 3	intermediate	B1	96	11,000–15,000	approx. 1,100
Level 4	upper intermediate	B2	112	15,000–19,000	approx. 1,700

For more information on the Collins COBUILD Grading Scheme, including a full list of the grammar structures found at each level, go to www.collinselt.com/readers/gradingscheme.

Also available online: Make sure that you are reading at the right level by checking your level on our website (www.collinselt.com/readers/levelcheck).

Gaius Julius Caesar

♦ ♦ ♦

100 BCE–44 BCE

the powerful Roman leader

From a young age I wanted to be a leader and a hero. I fought hard to gain control of many territories for Rome. I think it was my fate to become <u>dictator</u> of Rome.

◆ ◆ ◆

I was born on 12ᵗʰ July 100 <u>BCE</u>, in Rome in Italy. I am known as Julius Caesar but my first name was Gaius. Julius was my family's surname and Caesar was the name of the group of people we came from, our tribe. My mother's name was Aurelia and my father was called Gaius Caesar. He was the Governor of <u>Asia Minor</u> and although he came from an <u>aristocratic</u> Roman family, we were not rich. We were not poor either, but there were many people who were far wealthier than we were.

I had an enjoyable childhood playing and fighting with my friends. I learned to ride at a young age and developed a passion for horses and racing, and we had many competitions to see who was the fastest, most fearless rider. I knew that it was important to be educated but my father taught me that the most important thing was to know how to fight well. In our time, Rome had many enemies and I knew about all of them.

Rome was a republic, which meant that its rulers were elected by the people or their representatives. The government consisted of the Consuls, the Senate and the Assembly. At the head of the government were the Consuls. These were two people who were elected every year. The Consuls controlled the day-to-day working of the government and were the only people who could command the army. Below them was the Senate. This consisted of 300 men, called senators, who came from the <u>aristocracy</u>. They kept their positions for life and were chosen by the two Consuls. The Assembly was made up of all the ordinary men in Rome. They had the right to vote and to give speeches, and they chose the two Consuls.

My father taught me that political power and military power were connected and it was not possible to have one without the other. He also taught me that to survive, it was vital to gain the respect of ordinary people. These were the people who really had the power because they chose who was in charge of the government. His advice proved to be valuable in the future.

◆ ◆ ◆

My youth was a time of <u>civil war</u> in Rome, with two groups fighting for control. On the one side was a man called Gaius Marius, who was married to my father's sister, Julia. Marius was the leader of the Populares party. He represented the ordinary people of Rome and we supported him. On the other side was a general called Sulla, who was from an aristocratic background. Both sides fought violently and committed terrible acts of war but in 88 BCE, Sulla did something that nobody had done before. He led his army into Rome to try to take control of the city by force. The fighting continued.

Four years later, when I was 16 years old, my father died. Suddenly, as his eldest son, I became the leader of our family. At that time, my uncle Marius was in power, together with one of his revolutionary friends called Cinna. Cinna had a lovely daughter called Cornelia and we decided to get married. Later we had a daughter called Julia.

In 83 BCE, Marius and Cinna lost power to Sulla and life became dangerous for me. Sulla was afraid of the political power I had because of my wife's family's position in society. He ordered me to divorce her or he would take my property away from me. I refused and he added my name to a list of those who were going to be <u>executed</u>. There were already a lot of names on the list. In the beginning, my friends took me to a safe hiding place. I was lucky that I had powerful friends and family, and my mother's family in particular had enough influence with Sulla to get me an <u>appeal</u>, and then a <u>pardon</u>. In spite of my pardon, I decided not to return to Rome and I stayed away until Sulla died in 78 BCE.

During this time, I joined the Roman army. In 79 BCE, I was awarded a civic crown – a crown made of leaves – for saving the life of a citizen. After that I was sent by my commanding officer to a place called Bithynia in northern Anatolia (the country now known as Turkey) to <u>negotiate</u>

with the king to buy a <u>fleet</u> of ships. I returned to Rome in 78 BCE after Sulla died, and started working for the government as a lawyer. I discovered that I had a talent for public speaking and I soon developed a good reputation. I made many friends and also a number of enemies. But it was a group of pirates that took away my liberty.

On a visit to Greece in 75 BCE, I visited the island of Rhodes, where I was captured by pirates who demanded a <u>ransom</u> for my release. While we waited for the money to be found and sent, the pirates treated me reasonably well. I had decided that I would be in less danger if I was friendly with them and so I did my best to be pleasant. I joked that when they let me go, I would come back to find them, and would then kill them. They laughed and joked too but this is exactly what I did. Once I was free, I gathered together some ships and soldiers. We sailed back to the sea around Rhodes and found the pirates. This time, there was no laughing and joking. I wanted revenge and I also wanted to warn other pirates that kidnapping was not a good way for them to make money. We cut their throats and I think my message was received and understood.

In 74 BCE, while I was still travelling, Asia Minor was attacked by the King of Pontus, Mithradates VI. I quickly created a private army of my own men and began defending a few towns that had been attacked. This gave the Roman <u>commander</u> time to organize his army and attack Mithradates. News of my actions travelled fast and in 73 BCE, I was elected as a Military Tribune – an officer in the army with the power to command – and I led my men into battle with pride.

I returned home and discovered that after 15 years of marriage, my wife had died in childbirth. Family and friends tried to make me feel better but I knew that working hard was the only way I could forget my sadness. The Assembly elected me as the financial officer for Andalusia in Spain, which was a Roman territory. My aunt Julia died and before I left for Spain, I gave a speech at her funeral which reminded the ordinary people – the voters in the Assembly – of my connections to the <u>influential</u> Marius family.

◆ ◆ ◆

In 68 BCE, a <u>seat</u> became available in the Senate and I was selected to become one of the 300. I had not forgotten how important it was to have political power if I wanted to follow a military career. In 67 BCE, it was time for me to marry again. My second wife, Pompeia, was a granddaughter of Sulla but the marriage ended a few years later. In the meantime, my political and military duties continued to keep me busy. When I returned to Rome in 65 BCE, I was elected as the official responsible for games and entertainment. To me, keeping the ordinary people of Rome entertained and happy was an important role as it would make me popular with the voting members of the Assembly. Making myself popular, however, was very expensive and I was in debt. I became friendly with a man called Crassus, who was the richest man in Rome. He kindly paid my debts for me.

My efforts to please the people had not been a waste of money because in 62 BCE, I was elected Consul. I continued to look for ways to increase my power and I wanted to surround myself with influential people. One of these was

General Pompey – known as Pompey the Great – who had just succeeded in making Syria a Roman territory. In 60 BCE, I persuaded him and the rich Crassus to form a political partnership with me that would benefit us all. We later became known as the First Triumvirate but at the time our enemies used to call us 'the three-headed monster'.

In 61 BCE, I became Governor of Spain. Our territories, in far distant lands, brought Rome great riches. It made me realize that our empire should expand further. On my return, I was elected once more as Consul. In 59 BCE, when I was 40 years old, I married again. My third wife was a beautiful young woman called Calpurnia, whose father was a close friend of Crassus, and we celebrated our marriage with a grand ceremony. We didn't get the chance to spend much time together as news from the north suggested there was great trouble ahead. I was pleased, for wherever there was trouble, there was also opportunity.

In 58 BCE, I continued north with my army and became governor of northern Italy and southern France. My soldiers were well-trained and ready for battle. We defeated the armies we faced in what we called Gaul – France, Belgium, Switzerland, the Netherlands and Germany. It was not easy as we had to climb wild mountains and cross deep wide rivers. Also, feeding thousands of men needed organization and keeping them fit and ready for battle was essential.

By the year 55 BCE, we had reached the Belgian beaches. 32 kilometres across the water was Britain. This was a challenge for any military leader, particularly late in the summer when winter was not far away. We built 80 ships, and with 10,000 soldiers we set off. The waves and wind caused great difficulty for our men and some of them died on the voyage. We arrived in Britain and set up armed camps. The Britons were organized, but we made solid progress. The bad weather continued to make our lives almost impossible and we did not have enough supplies. I made the decision that we should go back to France until the winter was over. This would give us time to prepare for the next attack.

In the summer of 54 BCE, we invaded Britain again. I took 25,000 foot soldiers and 2,000 men on horseback but to our surprise, the big defence we had been expecting was not there. Once again our biggest enemy was nature. A terrible storm destroyed about 40 of our boats, but we managed to repair them and continued. We fought our way through the country and arrived at a place called Westminster. But news from France, where we had our main camp, was bad. It was necessary to return there, before winter arrived. So, to the surprise of the Britons, we took all our soldiers and travelled back across the sea. You may ask what was gained from the expedition. We had researched the territory and the local people, gathering information that would be useful in later invasions. We also learned about the chariots and lightweight boats the Britons used and we were able to adapt them for our own use.

The bad news in France was that local armies had joined forces under a new leader called Vercingetorix, who proved to be a tough opponent. Much blood was spilt on both sides, but my soldiers were so well-trained that we won. As a result, Rome ruled most of Gaul. During the winter of 52 BCE, I wrote a book called *The Gallic Wars* and while I was writing, news arrived from home that Crassus had died. While I was gaining new lands, Crassus had been my support in Rome.

The return journey to Rome was long and tiring but it was good to see our soldiers still held control of the lands we had captured. On my arrival, I noted many changes. Pompey, the third member of our little group, had gained victories and land in the east, but he wanted more power.

In Rome, he was planning a <u>rebellion</u> against me. He sent a message telling me to put my men under his command. This was an insult and a challenge to my authority. In 49 BCE, I told my army they had to fight for their lives and if they lost, they would be powerless under Pompey's control. As I led my soldiers over the River Rubicon, I knew that I was breaking the rule that Roman generals did not bring their armies into Rome.

A civil war was the result, and a fight to the death. If we were defeated, my generals and I would be executed. In 48 BCE, after bitter battles where Romans fought Romans, we defeated Pompey's army and Rome, like most of Europe, was at last under my command. Soon after my victory, news arrived from Egypt, where a civil war was also taking place. I decided that we should join in the fighting and make Egypt a Roman territory. Pompey's army – now weak – had also gone there. In 47 BCE, I set off with my army and arrived in Alexandria. On arriving, I heard that Pompey had been killed by King Ptolemy. When I met Ptolemy's <u>advisor</u>, Pothinus, I learned that the king was now also my enemy.

I needed to look for other support amongst the Egyptians and that is how I met Cleopatra, the sister of King Ptolemy. Cleopatra was at war with her brother and by joining forces with her, our armies defeated his. I could not rest though, because I had to make sure we kept control of each new territory we had won. I left 15,000 soldiers in Egypt and fought my way back home, gaining yet more lands for Rome. To celebrate, I wrote "veni, vidi, vici" – "I came, I saw, I <u>conquered</u>".

Julius Caesar's empire

GERMANY

BRITAIN

Atlantic
Ocean

Gaul

Cisalpine
Gaul

Transalpine
Gaul

FURTHER
SPAIN

NEARER
SPAIN

CORSICA

SARDINIA

ITALY

Rome

Illyricum

AFRICA

Africa
Nova

Sicily

Mediterranean
Sea

Thrace

Macedonia

Black Sea

Bithynia and Pontus

Asia

Crete

Cyrenaica

Cappadocia

Cilicia

Cyprus

SYRIA

Judaea

EGYPT

Areas within the Roman empire at the end of Caesar's rule

Back home, I realized that strong control was needed and my time was taken up planning a new future for Rome. The Senate gave me the power of a dictator. Some people in the Senate, who had supported Pompey, were unhappy that I was in a position of such power and complained but I didn't take them seriously. I should have done, because when my soldiers were absent, I was attacked by 60 of Pompey's supporters. They approached me from behind and they were armed with knives. I was stabbed 23 times and my blood ran down the steps of the Senate. It was the end of an era. I hoped the Romans would do something worthy with the <u>legacy</u> that I left behind me.

The Life of Julius Caesar

100 BCE	Gaius Julius Caesar was born in Rome, Italy.
88 BCE	The Roman general Sulla entered Rome with a Roman army to gain back power.
84 BCE	When Julius was 16, his father Gaius died. He remained close to his mother, Aurelia.
c. 84 BCE	Julius married Cornelia, the daughter of a revolutionary associate of Marius. She later had a daughter, Julia.
83 BCE	When Sulla gained control of Rome, he ordered Julius to divorce his wife, but he refused. Julius went into hiding.
78 BCE	After Sulla's death, Julius returned to Rome and entered the Government as a lawyer.
75 BCE	On a visit to Rhodes, Julius was kidnapped by pirates. Once released, he captured the pirates and executed them.
74 BCE	Julius gathered a private army to fight against the attacks on the Roman Empire of Mithradates VI, the King of Pontus.

c. 73 BCE	After he returned to Rome, Julius was elected to be a tribune for the military.
70 BCE–65 BCE	Both Cornelia and his aunt died. Julius was elected to the Senate. He married Pompeia, a granddaughter of Sulla. The marriage lasted a few years.
64 BCE	Pompey gained Syria as a Roman territory.
60 BCE	Julius persuaded Pompey and Crassus to join him in a political partnership known now as the First Triumvirate.
59 BCE	Julius got married for the third time to Calpurnia.
58 BCE	Julius was elected Consul. He travelled north to become Governor of northern Italy and southern France.
55 BCE	Julius made the first of his two invasions of Britain.
53 BCE	Crassus was killed at Carrhae, in Turkey, when the Parthians defeated his army.
52 BCE	The leader of the armies in France, Vercingetorix, defeated Julius, but was captured later in the year. Julius wrote *The Gallic War*.

49 BCE   Julius crossed the River Rubicon (the southern boundary of Gaul) with his army – and in doing so launched a civil war and became leader of Italy.

48 BCE–47 BCE   Julius defeated Pompey at Pharsalus, in Greece, and made himself master of the Roman world. Pompey was killed by King Ptolemy in Egypt. He met Cleopatra. Julius conducted a campaign in Asia Minor so quickly that he declared, "I came, I saw, I conquered".

44 BCE   Julius was murdered aged 55, in Rome. He was killed by opponents in the senate who stabbed him 23 times. Julius was declared a god in the Roman religion.

Queen
Elizabeth I

• ◆ •

1533–1603

the queen who ruled England for 45 years

My childhood had been a time of great fear, for both me and my country. When I became Queen of England, I wanted my people to experience peace, happiness and a greater sense of freedom. I think I was successful.

♦ ◆ ♦

I, Elizabeth Tudor, was the daughter of King Henry VIII and Anne Boleyn and I was born at Greenwich Palace, London, on 7th September 1533. My mother was my father's second wife – in total he was married six times – and I was his second daughter. His first child, my half-sister, Mary, was 17 when I came into the world. When my father wanted to marry my mother, he was already married to his first wife. The Pope – the head of the Catholic Church – refused to give him a divorce. Henry left the Catholic Church, declared himself the head of the Church of England – a <u>Protestant</u> church – and gave himself permission to get divorced.

After three years of marriage, my mother only had one child, myself. The marriage was not a happy one and my father hadn't got the son he really wanted. He wanted a male <u>heir</u> to become king after his own death. He blamed my mother for not giving him a son and decided to get married again. This meant that he had to find a way to become free from his current wife.

On 2nd May 1536, my mother was arrested for <u>treason</u> and several other crimes. It was widely believed, then and afterwards, that she was not guilty of any of the crimes she had been accused of, but on 19th May 1536, she was publicly <u>beheaded</u>. I was not even 3 years old. Eleven days later, my father married his third wife, Jane Seymour. Henry declared that I was no longer his heir, just as he had done with my sister, Mary, when he divorced her mother.

♦ ◆ ♦

Even before my mother died, I did not see much of my parents. I had my own household in a palace near London called Hatfield House, where I was looked after by a series of <u>governesses</u>. In 1537, my stepmother, Jane Seymour, gave birth to a boy, Edward, but she died twelve days later. My father now had his heir. After Edward's birth, my father felt secure that his son was going to become king, so he wrote in his <u>will</u> that my sister Mary and I should be the next heirs to the <u>throne</u> once again.

♦ ◆ ♦

My childhood was not a happy time and in 1547, when I was 14, my father died. I hoped things would improve, but they didn't. My brother, who was 9 years old, was <u>crowned</u> Edward VI. Sadly, he was only king for six years. Before he died in 1553, when he was 15, he chose his cousin Lady Jane Grey to be his heir. Edward's <u>advisors</u> did not want Britain to become a Catholic country again, so the fact that Lady Jane Grey was Protestant was important. My sister, Mary, was not happy when Lady Jane Grey was crowned because Mary thought that she, herself, should be queen. After just nine days, Lady Jane Grey's right to the throne was taken away after a <u>ruling</u> by the Privy Council – an organization that had the power to pass laws – and Mary became Queen of England.

Mary had been brought up as a Catholic and made England Catholic again. The country faced bitter conflict as there was much <u>opposition</u> to what she was doing. Anyone who <u>stood in her way</u> was <u>executed</u> for the crime of being Protestant. There were many others – more than 300 – who were killed, including Lady Jane Grey and her husband. My father's preferred method of <u>execution</u> had been to cut people's heads off but Mary's was to burn them alive. Mary soon became known as 'Bloody Mary'.

I remained Protestant and as I was Mary's legal heir, I was seen by her as being a threat. I was <u>imprisoned</u> in the <u>Tower of London</u> and I felt sure that I was going to be executed. However, after two months, I was released and was sent to live at the Royal Palace of Woodstock in Oxfordshire where I was allowed to have my own household. I was no longer a prisoner but I certainly wasn't free. I was constantly watched by my sister's spies.

◆ ◆ ◆

Not long after becoming queen, Mary married King Philip II of Spain and soon she was pregnant. This baby, not I, would be Mary's heir, and I was no longer a threat. I was released and I returned to live at my palace in Hatfield. However, Mary never gave birth and it was generally believed that her symptoms were caused by illness rather than pregnancy.

After five years of terror, as Mary continued to search for Protestants, the future of the country was looking rather bad and there was talk of <u>civil war</u>. In the autumn of 1558, news reached us that Mary, who was now 42, was unwell. On 17th November 1558, her death was announced. On that day, at the age of 25, I became Queen Elizabeth I of England.

♦ ◆ ♦

The night before my <u>coronation</u> on 15th January 1559, I stayed at the Palace of Westminster. This was a short distance from Westminster Abbey, where the ceremony was going to take place. The next morning, I walked from the palace to the abbey on a blue carpet that had been especially made for the occasion, and thousands of people came out into the streets to see me. After the ceremony was over, the carpet completely disappeared – not even the smallest sign of it was left. My people had torn it into little pieces so that each of them could go home with a souvenir of the day. I had arranged for a fantastic feast to be held with the best food, drink and entertainment that money could buy. I wanted the day I became Queen of England to be remembered as a marvellous celebration.

Now that there was no doubt that I, the only living child of Henry VIII, was the legal and <u>rightful</u> heir to the throne, <u>lords</u> and church leaders had to accept me as their queen. These were the same people who had been responsible for my imprisonment and <u>humiliation</u>. Now it was their turn to feel afraid as I was not only their queen, but Protestant, too. I was not a very religious person but I did not want the Pope to have more power in my country than I did. So one of my first tasks was to announce myself as Supreme Governor of the Church of England and later, in 1563, I created the <u>Anglican</u> Church.

Naturally this angered the Catholics and I realized that I had many enemies. I needed a Chief Advisor I could trust and I gave the position to a man called William Cecil. He managed the politics in Parliament, organized the finances and set up the secret police. As well as Cecil, I employed more than 600 people to help me rule the country and another 600, whose job was to control our expanding <u>empire</u>.

◆ ◆ ◆

One way for a foreign prince or king to gain incredible power was to marry the Queen of England and from the moment I became queen, I received many proposals of marriage. One of the first to propose was my dead sister's husband, King Philip II of Spain, who wanted to keep his political connection to England. He felt that because he had been married to my sister, he had the right to be king of England. I refused to marry him, which later had serious consequences.

In fact, I refused to marry anyone and I remained single my entire life. I never told anyone why I chose not to marry and there was much discussion and many rumours about the reason. Some people thought that I did not like the company of men, but this was not true. One of my closest friends was a man called Lord Robert Dudley, who became a member of the Privy Council. Even after his wife died, I decided not to marry him, for political reasons. We stayed close friends and he continued to play an important role in my government.

In 1562, I became ill with smallpox – a terrible disease – and everyone, including myself, thought that I was going to die. I recovered but the following year there was an outbreak in London of the bubonic plague, or the Black Death, as it was known. This was a truly awful disease that killed hundreds of thousands of people all across Europe. To try to keep us safe, I moved the <u>royal court</u> away from London to the town of Windsor and it was forbidden for all those who had been in London to visit us. If anyone ignored this, they were executed.

The queen of Scotland, known as Mary Queen of Scots, was my cousin. Many Catholics in England viewed Mary as the rightful heir to the English throne. They believed that my father's marriage to my mother had not been legal and that I was not the true heir and should not have been made queen. As a result, there were several attempts to kill me and make Mary queen. I was fully aware that Mary was a threat to me and I spent a considerable time thinking about how I could reduce the danger. In 1560, when Mary was 18 years old, her French husband died and she returned from France – where she had lived most of her life – to rule Scotland. Robert Dudley's wife also died in the same year and I thought it might be a good idea if he married Mary. To do this he needed to be a member of the <u>aristocracy</u>, so I gave him the title of Earl of Leicester and a large amount of land. However, he refused to marry her.

In 1565, Mary married a man called the Earl of Darnley but the marriage was not a happy one. Two years later Darnley was killed in an explosion and many people thought he had been murdered. Just three months later, Mary married a man called the Earl of Bothwell. Those who believed that Darnley had been murdered also believed that it was Bothwell who was responsible for his death. The Scottish aristocracy, already unhappy with Mary because she was a Catholic queen in a Protestant country, turned against her. In 1567, she was forced to give up her throne in favour of her one-year-old son, James. She was imprisoned in a place called Loch Leven Castle. Worried that she might be killed, Mary managed to escape from Scotland and asked me for protection.

When Mary came to England, I had to put her under <u>house arrest</u> because I needed to know what she was doing and who she was seeing. Two years later, my spies discovered another attempt – later named the Ridolfi Plot – to kill me and put Mary on my throne. I decided that I had to lock her away more securely. For the next 19 years she was closely guarded.

In 1586, a man called Anthony Babbington was planning a <u>rebellion</u> that would make Mary Queen of England in my place. The head of my secret police, Francis Walsingham, discovered the plans before Babbington could take action. As part of the investigation, it was discovered that Mary had been writing regularly to Babbington. This suggested very strongly that she was involved in the rebellion. My advisors persuaded me that Mary was always going be a threat to me and that I would only be safe if she were dead. I was not altogether happy about this but there seemed to be no alternative. Mary was accused of treason and to my regret, on 8th February 1587, when she was 44 years old, she was executed.

♦ ◆ ♦

In the meantime, I was extremely busy with other work. In 1570, the Pope excluded me from the Catholic Church and stated that Catholics under my rule were free to <u>worship</u>. Many priests were sent into England to try to persuade people to become Catholic. Although I was unwilling, the Pope's action gave my government no choice but to pass strict laws preventing this from happening and many Catholics were executed.

In 1562, an English sea captain – John Hawkins – began our involvement in the slave trade. He was joined a year later by another English captain called Francis Drake. They started catching people in Sierra Leone on the West African coast and selling them as slaves to the Spanish <u>colonists</u> in the Caribbean. Until this time, only Spanish slave <u>traders</u> had been allowed to do this work. The Spanish became angry that England was making money from this very profitable business.

In 1567, when Drake was bringing in a large number of slaves for the first time, the Spanish attacked Drake's ships and destroyed nearly all of them. Only two ships were left. The Spanish became enemies to Drake, and they thought he was a dangerous pirate. In 1572, Drake came back to England with two ships full of treasure he had stolen from the Spanish. I have to admit that I did not have a great deal of control over Drake's actions but I was not unhappy with what he achieved for his country. The Spanish, however, were not at all pleased.

In 1577, I sent Drake off on a secret journey around the world, so he could not only import gold, <u>pearls</u> and spices, but also find new territories – some of which he took away from the Spanish – to add to our empire. He was the first Englishman to sail right round the world and when he came back in 1580, I <u>knighted</u> him for his efforts.

While Drake was making the Spanish colonists angry, we were fighting other battles closer to home. The Netherlands were being ruled by King Philip II of Spain but really wanted to be independent. They had been Protestant and wanted to go back to their own religion. A friendly agreement existed between them and us and when, in 1585, a rebellion began there, I sent an English army commanded by Robert Dudley to help them fight. The rebellion was successful and the Dutch Republic was formed.

In 1587, my spies in Spain sent reports that the Spanish were building a huge navy, which they called the Armada. King Philip's intention was, they said, to invade England, kill me and become king of England. After we learnt of Philip's plan, Francis Drake went to Cádiz in Spain, where the ships were being built, and destroyed 30 of them. The following year, in 1588, Phillip, sent 130 ships – the Armada – to the coast of Britain. We had in total 197 ships, all armed and ready for war. With Sir Francis Drake in command of all the English ships, the Spanish Armada was defeated, but the war with Spain continued for another fifteen years.

◆ ◆ ◆

In the early 1590s, there were about 75,000 people living in London. Suddenly, in 1593, the Black Death returned, rapidly killing over 20,000 people. This was an enemy that we could not fight, but there were other threats that were not so deadly. We were having constant problems with Catholic rebellions. I made it a serious crime to go to a Catholic church and people who did not attend Church of England services could be punished.

In Ireland, in 1594, a rebellion began that lasted until 1603. In 1599, I sent an army to defeat them, putting a close friend of mine, Robert Devereaux, the Earl of Essex, in command. When Robert <u>betrayed</u> me by starting his own rebellion against me, I was shocked and terribly upset. In 1601, he was found guilty of treason and was executed.

Fighting was expensive and so I encouraged the development of businesses overseas. Thanks to the river Thames, the port of London was busier than it had ever been, as traders came from all over the world to do business with us. In 1600, I gave permission for The East India Company to be created. This was a private company that brought goods back from the East Indies – India and the Middle East. At the time, the Dutch had a <u>monopoly</u> on the spice trade and I wanted Britain to be part of what was a very profitable business.

Apart from fighting wars and making money, I tried to be involved in other exciting activities. I had heard about a brilliant young man called William Shakespeare who was busy writing plays and I even went to the theatre to see the first performance of a play called *A Midsummer Night's Dream*. It was most enjoyable.

While I was queen, I wanted my people to know me and have the chance to see me face-to-face. In the summer months, when London was hot and uncomfortable, I liked to travel around the country and I went on more than 25 such trips. When the weather allowed it, I often rode on horseback instead of in a carriage. This personal contact was partly responsible for my popularity, but life wasn't all about fame and admiration.

By 1601, there was serious poverty throughout the country and I knew it was time for me to do something about it. I always tried to do my best for my people – I was called the Good Queen Bess by many. Before my father's time, the Catholic Church had looked after the poor, but now this was not happening in an organized way. The Poor Law of 1601 made sure that money raised through taxes went to providing food, housing, clothing and medical help to the poorest people in every area.

In 1603, I became ill myself, with blood poisoning, and on 24th March, I died at my home in Richmond Palace. I had made England a rich and powerful country and the time I spent as queen was later called The Golden Age.

The Life of Queen Elizabeth I

1533   Elizabeth Tudor was born in Greenwich
        Palace, England on 7th September. She was
        the daughter of King Henry VIII.

1536   Elizabeth's mother, Anne Boleyn, was
        accused and found guilty of treason as well
        as other crimes. She was executed and King
        Henry VIII married Jane Seymour.

1537   Jane Seymour died after her son Edward
        was born. It was declared that Elizabeth
        was no longer a legal heir. She moved to a
        palace near London called Hatfield House.

1547   King Henry VIII died. Elizabeth's half-
        brother became King Edward VI of
        England. Elizabeth lived with Katherine
        Parr and her new husband, Thomas
        Seymour.

1553   King Edward VI died. He had declared
        Lady Jane Grey his heir, and she was Queen
        for just nine days. Elizabeth's sister, Mary,
        replaced her as Queen of England.

1554   Lady Jane and her husband were executed.
        Elizabeth was imprisoned in the Tower of
        London for eight weeks on false charges.
        When she was released, Elizabeth was sent to
        Woodstock and was kept under house arrest.

1555   England returned to Catholicism, and being a Protestant was a crime. Queen Mary earned the name "Bloody Mary".

1558   Queen Mary I died and Elizabeth, aged 25, became Queen. England became Protestant.

1559   Elizabeth was crowned Queen of England.

1562   She nearly died, after becoming ill with smallpox.

1563   The Anglican Church was established. The Bubonic Plague broke out in London and Elizabeth moved her court to Windsor Castle.

1568   Mary Queen of Scots escaped from Scotland and Elizabeth imprisoned her.

1570   Elizabeth decided she would never marry. She was forced to leave the Catholic Church.

1571   The Ridolfi Plot, a plan to assassinate Elizabeth and put Mary Queen of Scots in power was uncovered.

1575   A friendly agreement was made between England and the Netherlands.

1580 After a three-year voyage round the world,
      Francis Drake returned to England after
      claiming territories for England. The
      following year, Elizabeth awarded him a
      knighthood.

1586 The Babbington Plot was uncovered.
      Anthony Babbington planned to kill
      Elizabeth and to replace her with Mary
      Queen of Scots. Mary was put on trial.

1587 Mary Queen of Scots was executed for her
      involvement in the Babbington Plot.

1588 England was at war with Spain. The
      English navy defeated the Spanish Armada.
      War between England and Spain continued.

1593 It became a crime to attend Catholic church
      services and people who did not attend
      Church of England services were punished.

1601 Elizabethan Poor Law made local churches
      responsible for caring for people who
      needed help.

1603 Elizabeth died, aged 69, in Richmond
      Palace, England.

George Washington

♦ ♦ ♦

1732–1799

the first president of the United States of America

When I was a boy, America was a British <u>colony</u> without its own power. By the time I was President of the United States of America, we had our own government. We had our own <u>constitution</u> but most of all, we had independence.

◆ ◆ ◆

I was born on 22nd February 1732, in Westmoreland County in the state of Virginia. My mother, Mary, was my father's second wife and I was the oldest of their six children. I also had two older half-brothers and a half-sister, the children of my father and his first wife, Jane, who died in 1729. Both my parents were the children of <u>colonists</u>. My great-grandfather, John Washington, had come to Virginia from England in 1657 and had acquired land where he grew <u>tobacco</u> and owned slaves, who worked on the <u>plantation</u>. My father, Augustine, had <u>inherited</u> the tobacco plantation, and we were wealthy in a modest way. Virginia and other colonies in the South were 'slave societies' where landowners who kept slaves had become the upper class. The economy had been built using slaves to work in the fields and also to work inside the fine houses as servants.

In 1735, we moved to a plantation on the Potomac river called Little Hunting Creek, which was later renamed Mount Vernon. Three years later, leaving Hunting Creek to be run by my older brother Lawrence, we moved again, to a plantation called Ferry Farm where I grew up. From the age of 7 until I was 15, I had lessons at home. My father died in 1743, when I was 11 years old, and he left Ferry Farm to me and Mount Vernon to Lawrence. Things became more difficult for us financially.

My older brothers had been sent to school in England but after my father's death, there was not enough money for me to go to England, so my education continued at home. I was not taught Latin or Greek or a modern foreign language as was normal for the son of a gentleman and it wasn't possible for me to attend college of any kind. I always felt embarrassed by my lack of education, which I tried to make up for by reading as much as possible. I also spent a great deal of my time working in the fields and I learnt everything there was to know about growing tobacco and running a plantation. Lawrence became like a father to me and I spent a lot of time with his family at Mount Vernon. His wife, Anne Fairfax, came from a wealthy family and she taught me how to behave like a Virginian gentleman. Anne's family were very influential and she introduced me to many important people.

In 1748, when I was 16, I went with a group of surveyors to the western part of Virginia. Their job was to examine areas of land, measure them and make a map for potential buyers of the land. I learnt how to do this myself and the following year, with the help of <u>Lord</u> Fairfax, Anne's father, I was made the official surveyor of Culpeper County in Virginia, which was a good, well-paid job. I also learnt the most valuable skill of knowing which pieces of land were potentially valuable.

Surveying kept me very busy for the next two years until my brother, Lawrence, became ill with tuberculosis – a nasty disease affecting mainly the lungs. I took him to Barbados, an island in the British West Indies, thinking that the climate there would help him, but it didn't. He got worse. I also became ill, with a serious disease called smallpox, so we came back home to Virginia. Smallpox had been brought to North America by the first Europeans and also by the slaves from some parts of Africa. It was known that if you had been ill with smallpox and survived, you were immune to further attacks of it. This meant that it was impossible for you to ever become sick again with the same disease. I recovered, but in 1752 Lawrence died.

◆ ◆ ◆

Shortly after my brother's death, I became an officer in Virginia's Militia, which was an army made up of non-professional soldiers and officers – men who normally did other jobs and only joined the army in times of war – and was loyal to the British King. At this time, parts of America were British colonies and were ruled with its laws. Other

parts belonged to the French, who were trying to increase their territories in America. One of the places they were trying to gain control of was Ohio County which already belonged to the British in Virginia, and there was fighting between the two nations.

In 1754, under the command of a British general called Braddock, we attacked the French but unfortunately the battle was a disaster for us and Braddock himself was killed. Despite this, my <u>superiors</u> thought that I had acted well and I was made <u>Commander</u> of Virginia's army. For the next three years, we fought constantly against the French. In 1758, in the Forbes Expedition, we got control of Ohio County and peace returned to Virginia. I resigned from the army and went back to Mount Vernon where I entered the world of politics.

The Virginia Burgesses had been created 140 years before. These were types of local government, the first to be created in the British American colonies. Members were elected by male landowners over the age of 21. In 1761, I was elected, first for Frederick County and then I won the seat for Fairfax County, which I kept until 1775.

On 6th January 1759, I got married. My wife, Martha Dandridge Custis, was a wealthy widow with two small children but we did not have any children together. When we got married, we were both 27 years old. It was the start of a new and very busy life as I was now responsible for running Martha's plantation as well as Mount Vernon where we lived. In 1754, my brother's widow had remarried and was no longer living at Mount Vernon. I rented the plantation from her until her own death in 1761, when I inherited it.

At that point, I was still a loyal colonist, not a revolutionary and I concentrated on developing the plantations. In 1764, we switched from growing tobacco to growing wheat and I made sure I was aware of and applied all the new farming methods. As a politician, however, things were not as satisfying. The British were making life difficult for the colonists as the laws made in Britain were not suitable for us, and respect for the British was starting to decline. It was becoming obvious that we needed our own government.

In 1773, the British government put new high taxes on imported products, one of them being tea. When shiploads of the tea arrived in America, most of it was sent back to where it had come from, but in Boston, the governor refused to allow the tea to be returned. A group of men went on board the ships, found the tea and threw it all into the sea. The event was later named the Boston Tea Party. The British government responded by closing the port of Boston until all the tea had been paid for and by passing a series of laws. These laws seriously limited the powers of the colony of Massachusetts to govern itself. The Boston Tea Party had been the first serious rebellious act against the British government and the resulting action by the British further angered the colonists.

In 1774, the first Continental Congress was held to discuss how we could act together against the British government. From the thirteen colonies in America, 12 sent representatives – only Georgia did not – and I was one of the 56 people who was elected to attend. We produced the Declaration of Rights which stated that America did not have to follow decisions made by the parliament in Britain about things that happened only in America. We agreed that the Congress would meet again in May 1775.

By this time, the revolution had begun and there was considerable fighting. The Continental Army was created and I was made Commander-in-Chief of it. My previous military experience impressed the Congress. When I was elected to be the commander, I crossed the line between being a colonist and being a revolutionary. Legally, I was guilty of <u>treason</u> against the British, but I needed to fight for what I felt was right. Training and organizing the men became my first priority, despite the personal danger to myself. Soldiers came from all 13 colonies to join the army, but before long it was clear that we had a more powerful enemy closer to home, and that was smallpox.

I knew that if there was an outbreak of the disease in the army, our numbers would be seriously reduced. In Boston, where we were based, an outbreak happened that autumn. I heard rumours that the British had deliberately sent people with smallpox to mix with our soldiers so that the disease would spread through the army, but there was no way of proving it was true. I decided that any soldier who showed even the slightest symptom of smallpox should be kept securely away from the others. And there was a way, called inoculation, that I could make all the soldiers in the army immune to smallpox, like I was.

It was possible, with skilled medical help, to make people ill with a weak form of the disease. They were sick for about a month and then recovered, knowing that they would never get smallpox again. However, although I was in great favour of inoculation, I did not want my entire army to be out of action for a whole month at a time when it should be fighting. I compromised and by 1779, I made sure that every new soldier had been inoculated.

◆ ◆ ◆

The Congress had decided that America would have its own currency so paper money was printed, and we already had our own postal system. On 4th July 1776, the Declaration of Independence was signed by all the delegates – except for me as I was away – and made public. It explained what we doing and why we wanted to free ourselves from the British. The Declaration was sent to my battlefield headquarters in New York, where I was based with my army and on 6th July 1776, I proudly announced it to my officers.

One of the main messages in the Declaration was that all men are created equal and that they have a few unquestionable rights such as life, liberty and the <u>pursuit</u> of happiness. Since the age of 11, I had owned slaves who had no rights because they were not citizens. They could not own property, could not vote, were not allowed even the most basic education and of course were not free. My wealth depended on the work done by slaves and in my youth it was something that I did not question. As I grew older, I began to realize that <u>slavery</u> was wrong and in my <u>will</u> I stated that all the slaves I owned were to be given their freedom on my death.

One of the first battles of the revolution that we won against the British was the Siege of Boston in 1775, which was a truly encouraging victory for us. During the next two years, we lost in New York at the Battle of Long Island and then again in 1777, when we were defeated in Pennsylvania at the Battle of Brandywine. There followed a long series of battles, some of which we lost. Our victory at Saratoga in October 1777 was the turning point when we realized we probably were going to win the war. In 1781, in the final major battle of the revolution, with the help of the French army, we beat the British in the Battle of Yorktown in Virginia. On 19th October 1781, the commander of the British army, General Cornwallis, <u>surrendered</u>. It took another two years before the war was over. That happened on 3rd September 1783 when the Treaty of Paris was signed, stating that the United States was free and independent of the British in every way.

We had been at war for eight years and I believed that I had done my duty and achieved my aim of freeing America from British rule. I wanted to go home to Mount Vernon and return to my life as a gentleman farmer. I did return, but in 1787 I was asked to take part in the Constitutional Convention in Philadelphia to head the committee that was working on the constitution. The people there tried to persuade me that I was the most suitable man to become our new country's first president. I wasn't sure, but on 7th January 1789, at the age of 57, I was elected President, with John Adams as Vice President. In 1790, I chose a place on the Potomac River to become our capital – it was named after me – and I created the first National Bank. Then I was elected a second time in 1792, but refused to be a candidate for a third time. In 1796, I gave my Farewell Address where I said goodbye to my country and gave advice as to how they should continue to govern.

In 1797, I went back home to Mount Vernon. I was quite tired from my life in politics and before that as a military man, but I focused on developing my farm and spent my last days happily working there. On 14th December 1799, I died aged 67, but I had had the most satisfying life. More satisfying to me was knowing that after my death, my loyal, hard-working slaves would be free men and women. I knew that they would not have the same rights as white citizens, but I hoped that in the future they would have. To me, freeing my own slaves was the beginning of this process.

The Life of George Washington

1732   George was born on 22nd February in
        Westmoreland, Virginia. He was the first of
        six children born to Augustine Washington
        and his second wife, Mary.

1735   The family moved to Little Hunting Creek
        Plantation on the Potomac River.

1738   George and his family moved to Ferry Farm
        on the Rappahannock River, Virginia.

1739   George was educated at home. He spent his
        spare time working on the plantation.

1743   When George was 11, his father died.

1748   George travelled with a surveying party to
        Virginia's western territory.

1749   At the age of 17, George became the official
        surveyor of Culpeper County, Virginia.

1751   George went to Barbados with his brother,
        Lawrence, who was ill. George got smallpox
        and they returned to Mount Vernon.

1752   George's brother, Lawrence, died.

1753–1754   George was an officer in the Virginia
             Militia. The French tried to take control of
             the Ohio Territory.

1755   George became commander of the Virginia army. He was the senior <u>advisor</u> to the British General, Edward Braddock.

1758   After the Forbes Expedition, George resigned from the army and returned home. He entered politics and was elected to Virginia's House of Burgesses.

1759   George married Martha Dandridge Custis. He became one of the richest landowners in Virginia.

1761   George inherited Mount Vernon after the death of Lawrence's wife.

1764   He changed his main crop from tobacco to wheat.

1774   George attended the First Virginia Convention, where he was elected to go to the First Continental Congress.

1775   George was chosen to be the Commander in Chief of the Continental Army. The Siege of Boston marked the beginning of the American Revolutionary War.

1776   The *Declaration of Independence* was signed.

1777–1778   George's army was defeated at the Battle of Brandywine but they won the Battle of Monmouth.

1779   George inoculated his soldiers against smallpox, which saved thousands of lives.

1781   George led his army to victory at the Battle of Yorktown.

1783   The British retreated and George led his army into New York City. The Treaty of Paris was signed and the war ended. George resigned from the army.

1787   George was elected as President of the Constitutional Convention.

1789   George was elected the first President of the United States.

1790   George chose the place for the nation's permanent capital, which was named after him.

1792   George was elected for a second term as President.

1796   George published his *Farewell Address,* which was also issued as a public letter.

1797   He returned, with his family, to Mount Vernon.

1799   On 14th December, George Washington died at Mount Vernon, aged 67. In his last will, he arranged for his slaves to be freed.

King Louis XVI

♦ ♦ ♦

1754–1793

the last king of France

I was very young and inexperienced when I became king. I wanted my people to be happy but I didn't know how to give them what they needed. At the time of my death, the French Revolution was turning France into a completely different country.

◆ ◆ ◆

I was born on 23rd August 1754 at the Palace of Versailles, approximately 20 kilometres away from the city of Paris. My full name was Louis Auguste and I was given the title of Duc de Barry. I was the grandson of the King of France, King Louis XV of the <u>House</u> of Bourbon. My father, also called Louis, was the Dauphin of France – the Dauphin was the <u>heir</u> to the <u>throne</u>, and was usually the oldest son of the king – and my mother was Marie Josèphe of Saxony. My parents weren't very interested in me but they paid a lot of attention to my older brother, Louis, Duc de Bourgogne, who was next in line to the throne after my father. I was a healthy child and I enjoyed hunting and other outdoor activities. From 1760, when I was 6 years old, my education was taken care of by a man called the Duc de La Vauguyon and I was taught religion, astronomy, physics, history and Latin by a number of aristocratic tutors. I was also good at modern languages and became quite fluent in Italian and English.

Being heir to the throne of France was no protection against the often fatal diseases that surrounded us. In 1761, my brother became ill with a horrible but very common disease called tuberculosis, which affected the lungs and sometimes other parts of the body. Later that year when he was 9 years old, he died. In 1765, my father died from the same illness and two years later, my mother followed him to the grave, also because of tuberculosis.

At the age of 9, I became the new Dauphin – when my grandfather died, I would become King of France. At the time in Paris, the average life expectancy – the age when most people die – was 29 and so when I was 15, it was time for me to marry. Royalty and the aristocracy did not marry for love. Marriage was an agreement, a legal contract that would benefit the families or countries of both the bride and groom. It was arranged that I would marry a 14-year-old girl called Marie Antoinette, the Archduchess of Habsburg in Austria. She was the daughter of the Holy Roman Emperor Francis I and was also my second cousin. The House of Habsburg was one of the most important royal houses in Europe and it was beneficial for them to have a daughter who was married to the future King of France. France had been at war with Prussia and a marriage between our two countries was a way of ensuring peace. Neither Marie Antoinette nor I were actually present at our wedding. In May 1770, we were married by proxy, which meant that we each had a legal representative who took our place. I finally met Marie Antoinette when she came to live at Versailles. I liked her, but we were not very close and our first child was not born until eight years after our wedding.

I had been very well educated in academic subjects but I was very shy and nobody had really taught me how to be charming or how to behave in a way that was socially acceptable. Until my brother died, nobody thought that I would be king and my education had not covered any of the skills I would need. I didn't know how to talk about finance or politics and I had no idea how to even begin any kind of <u>negotiation</u>. I was used to spending my days hunting in the grounds of Versailles or playing at my hobby which was making and fixing locks. In 1774, when my grandfather died and I became King, I was totally unprepared.

◆ ◆ ◆

French society was divided into three groups called Estates. The First Estate consisted of priests and religious leaders. They controlled about 10 per cent of the land but were only one per cent of the population. They were very wealthy and made most of their money from rents, which were collected from the people living and working on their land. As well as paying rent, these people had to pay a ten per cent tax on whatever profit they made from the land. The tax was <u>officially</u> for 'Church expenses' but this was a phrase with many <u>interpretations</u>. There was no doubt that some of the money was spent on maintaining the expensive lifestyle of the members of the First Estate. The Second Estate was the aristocracy, which made up two per cent of the population. These people had <u>inherited</u> their land and lived mainly on the money paid to them in rent. They owned 25 per cent of the land in France. The Third Estate was the rest of France – the 97 per cent who had few rights and no political power and therefore no hope of changing a situation which to them seemed extremely unfair.

When I became king, I inherited a country which was deeply in debt and full of misery. We had fought in the Seven Years War (1756-1763) against Prussia and Britain, which had been very expensive, especially considering we were defeated. My grandfather and the kings before him had greatly overspent on expensive entertainment and <u>luxurious</u> lifestyles. France was an absolute <u>monarchy</u>, which meant that it was the king who had to make all the decisions and rule the country. This was unlike other places, Britain, for example, which had a government that was also responsible for passing laws. Even though my grandfather officially had all the power, he had many <u>advisors</u> who often managed to convince him to do what they wanted, instead of what was right and good for France. In spite of, or maybe because of my inexperience, I had great plans for my country and wanted to try to make it a fairer society.

After I was <u>crowned</u> at the Cathedral in Reims in 1774, I wanted to make several changes. France was a Catholic country but I thought that people of other religions should be able to <u>worship</u> freely and have the same rights as Catholics. I also wanted to remove some of the taxes the poor had to pay and give them better <u>civil rights</u>. These proposed changes threatened both the church and the aristocracy who tried, successfully, to prevent me from making them. The only effect my proposals had, in the end, was to make me unpopular, and my wife, too, was not well-liked. The people were suspicious of our marriage because Marie Antoinette came from a Prussian background and we had been at war with Prussia not long before. She was also unpopular because she liked spending a great deal of money – money that we did not have.

In 1776, when the Americans declared their Independence from the British, I supported them and sent French armies to help them fight. We had already been fighting the British in America, with the help of American Indians, for control of some of the territories there and we were struggling to pay for our involvement. I knew that I was going to have difficulty organizing my country's finances, so I had made a man called Jean-Frédéric Phelypeaux my chief advisor. It was his idea to borrow large amounts of money from other nations, which greatly added to our own country's debt.

♦ ◆ ♦

In 1778, our first daughter, Marie Thérèse Charlotte was born, followed two years later by our son, Louis Joseph Xavier François. It was also the year in which American and French armies defeated the British in the Battle of Yorktown. In 1783, the war in America officially ended with the Treaty of Paris, as the British government accepted America's independence. Unfortunately, the treaty also meant that France had lost a large amount of land in America, too.

It was decided that the only way we could stop being in debt was to raise the amount of tax people had to pay and for the first time, people from the First and Second Estates had to start paying tax. It was a move that did not help me to become more popular. In the meantime, our third and fourth children were born. Sadly, out of the four children, only one lived to adulthood.

I had not given up my wish to make other religions legal and in 1787, I signed the Edict of Versailles which gave people of other religions the same rights as Catholics. Two years later, we produced a document called *The Declaration of the Rights of Man and of the Citizen*. Although women were not mentioned in the document, it said that 'Men are born free and equal in rights'. To me that meant natural rights to security, property, liberty and life. The role of government was to protect those rights. The First and Second Estates protested, as giving rights to the Third Estate threatened their own lifestyle and source of income. I was advised that it was time for a political meeting with representatives of all three Estates. I was not sure this was the best action to take because I was King and only I had the right to rule and make decisions. However, I agreed that it was the best option and to the surprise of my people, an Estates General Meeting was called on 5th May 1789.

The last time such a meeting had been called was in 1614, but unfortunately, the talks did not go as I had planned and were not a success. In the Third Estate were also all the <u>middle classes</u> – people who had their own businesses

The family of King Louis XVI

but were not members of the aristocracy or the church and who felt they were being ignored. They were demanding that normal citizens should be able to vote for the people ruling the country. About 1,000 representatives were at the talks but they could not agree among themselves. I was afraid that the Third Estate would start causing serious problems and so I decided they should not be allowed any further part in our discussions. In answer to this, the Third Estate set up their own group which they called the National Assembly. They declared their intention to create a <u>constitution</u>. Everyone in Paris wanted to be involved in making the new constitution and they began complaining and protesting about what they thought was wrong with society. The people were becoming increasingly angry and were starting to demonstrate in the streets. I had to send in soldiers to keep order, which just made the people even more furious and there was more violence.

This was obviously a situation that I could not allow to continue and on 20th June, I closed the Salles des États, where the Third Estate had their meetings. I didn't realize that my actions would start a revolution. On 14th July, the Bastille prison – where all the weapons were kept – was attacked by wild, angry people, who set up a revolutionary government. A rumour, which was not true, had been started, claiming that the aristocratic <u>lords</u> were going to murder the poor people on their lands. Instead of doing nothing, and tired of being afraid, the poor decided to take action. Violence spread across the country as aristocratic families were attacked and killed and their lands and riches taken away from them. In August, the Third Estate declared that the First and Second Estates should start paying taxes and they also published their Declaration of Rights. They demanded that I and my family should come to Paris to face them and accept their National Assembly. In October, we did come to Paris, after a large violent group of people threatened to attack us at Versailles, but it became very clear that we were not safe in Paris either.

In June 1791, I decided that my family should try to escape by leaving France. We decided we would be safe in Austria, where my wife's family were, and we started our journey. However, we were discovered, caught and brought back as prisoners to the Tuileries Palace in Paris. Many aristocrats were being guillotined – killed by a machine with a sharp blade that cut off their heads – in the Place de la Concorde in the middle of Paris and I knew that it wouldn't be long before the same happened to me and my family. I was right. I was accused and found guilty of <u>treason</u> and on 21st January 1793, I was led out for <u>execution</u>. No words could save me and my only hope was that the murderers would not kill my family, too. The revolution could remove the royal family, but not the history and tradition we left behind us. As the guillotine came down, I shouted to the crowd 'Vive La France'.

The Life of King Louis XVI

1754   Louis Auguste de France was born at the Palace of Versailles and was given the title of Duc de Barry at birth. His father was Louis, Dauphin of France and his mother was Marie-Josèphe of Saxony. Louis was also the grandson of Louis XV of France.

1760   Louis received a strict education from the Duc de La Vauguyon.

1761   His older brother, Louis, Duc de Bourgogne, died aged 9.

1765   Louis's father, the Dauphin of France, died. At the age of 11, Louis became the new Dauphin.

1767   His mother, Marie-Josèphe of Saxony, died.

1770   At the age of 15, Louis married Marie Antoinette, the 14-year-old Habsburg Archduchess.

1774   After the death of his grandfather, Louis XV, 19-year-old Louis was crowned King Louis XVI at the Cathedral, in Reims. He appointed Jean-Frédéric Phélypeaux, Comte de Maurepas, as his chief advisor.

1776   Louis actively supported American independence from Great Britain, during the American Revolutionary War. However, the cost of war put a major financial strain on the French economy.

1778   Louis's first child, Marie Thérèse Charlotte, was born.

1780   In America, Louisville, Kentucky was created and named in honour of Louis.

1781   A second son, Louis Joseph Xavier François was born. The Siege of Yorktown occurred, where American and French troops defeated the British Army.

1783   The Treaty of Paris was signed and ended the American Revolutionary War between Great Britain and the United States of America.

1785   The third son, Louis Charles Capet, the future Dauphin, was born.

1786   Their fourth child, Sophie Hélène Béatrix was born. Sadly, she died before her first birthday.

1787   Louis signed the Edict of Versailles, which allowed people of other religions the same rights as Catholics. Two years later, a document was produced and detailed the rights of man. It was called *The Declaration of the Rights of Man and of the Citizen*.

1789   Louis Joseph, the second son, died aged 7. The Estates–General was formed to correct the Government's financial crisis. The Third Estate announced a National Assembly. Louis responded by closing the meeting place of the Third Estate, the Salles des États. The French Revolution was beginning. The attack on the Bastille happened on 14th July.

1791   Louis tried, unsuccessfully, to escape with his family. The attempt is known as the 'Royal Flight to Varennes'.

1792   Louis was accused and found guilty of high treason before the National Convention.

1793   On 21st January, Louis XVI, aged 38, was executed under the guillotine, at the Place de la Concorde. Nine months later, Marie Antoinette was also executed. Louis Charles, who was the dauphin, became Louis XVII at the age of 8, but never had any power as King. He died in prison two years later. Louis XVI's daughter, Marie Thérèse Charlotte, was imprisoned for three years.

Winston Churchill

◆ ◆ ◆

1874–1965

the Prime Minister who led Britain to
victory in the Second World War

I had many roles in life. Some were political, some were military. I had many friends and even more enemies, but I am best remembered as being the cigar-smoking Prime Minister who led Britain to victory in the Second World War.

◆ ◆ ◆

I was born two months early on 30th November 1874, at my parents' home, Blenheim Palace, near Oxford in England. My father, Sir Randolph, came from an <u>aristocratic</u> family, the Dukes of Marlborough, and it was a family tradition for the men to become officers in the British army. My full name was Winston Leonard Spencer-Churchill, but like my father, I used the surname Churchill in my professional life. My mother, whose name was Jennie, was born in the USA and was the beautiful daughter of a millionaire. When I was between the ages of 2 and 6, we lived in Dublin in Ireland because of my father's job.

I didn't see very much of my parents – this was not pleasant, but not uncommon either in aristocratic families. My <u>nanny</u>, Elizabeth Everest, was far closer to me than my family and I loved her as if she were my mother. I stayed in touch with her until she died in 1895, when I was 21 years old. I was educated at home by a <u>governess</u> until I was sent to <u>boarding school</u> at the age of 8. I felt unloved by my parents who did not come to visit me, despite the fact that I wrote to them and asked them to. Even in the holidays I didn't see much of them. Perhaps as a result, I developed speech problems, a <u>lisp</u> and a <u>stutter</u>. I survived school but I can't say that I enjoyed it or that I was a good pupil. School seemed so dull compared to what was happening in the world. I saw the arrival of electricity, and the telephone, which stopped faraway places from being so far away. The most important lesson I learnt at school was the ability to stand up for myself, something that was of great use to me all my life.

In 1883, I left school and had to face the outside world. Coming from a military family, I felt that I should also <u>serve</u> my country, so I applied to the Royal Military College, at Sandhurst. I passed the entry exams on my third attempt and enrolled in the Cavalry – the group of soldiers in the army that ride horses. In 1895, after two years of hard training, I became an officer. It was a great achievement and one which even my parents recognized. The pay, however, was rather low and I was not able to afford the kind of lifestyle I was used to when my family had been supporting me.

The annual salary was £300 and I estimated that I needed at least another £500 in order to live as well as the officers around me did.

After seven months, I was allowed some time off and instead of relaxing, I wanted action. A London newspaper, the Daily Graphic asked me to go to Cuba, where there had been a <u>coup</u>, and send back reports. That is how I started as a journalist and, although it was dangerous, I loved it. I also discovered that I loved smoking Havana cigars, and so I started a habit that lasted all my life.

In 1896, I was sent by the military to Bombay in India (now known as Mumbai), which was part of the British <u>empire</u>. Here I faced a completely new kind of life with the heat, poverty, poor housing, and the <u>sanitation</u> problems. Among what seemed like chaos to us, we tried to establish order and education.

In 1897, there was fighting between the British and <u>tribesmen</u> in the Mamund Valley, in the north-west of the country where British India joined Afghanistan. Unlike many British soldiers who were killed, I was lucky enough to escape and I wrote about what I had experienced. For *The Story of the Malakand Field Force* I was paid £600, twice what I was earning each year as an officer.

The British Empire was under attack in many places and in 1898, my <u>regiment</u> was sent to Egypt to join forces there to fight to reclaim Sudan. The Battle of Omdurman lasted just five hours but it was absolutely thrilling. As well as fighting in the army, I was also reporting for *The Morning Post* and when I returned in 1899, I wrote *The River War*, describing the British victory over the Sudanese soldiers. In the same year, I resigned from the army as I was becoming interested in politics. There were elections and I was the candidate for the <u>Conservative Party</u> in Oldham, near Manchester in the north of England. Despite a strong campaign, I was unsuccessful and the <u>Labour</u> candidate won the <u>seat</u>.

As I was not involved in politics, I was now free to develop my career as a journalist and was still working as a war reporter for *The Morning Post*. On 12th October 1899, the second Boer War started between the British and the Boers – the Dutch <u>settlers</u> in South Africa – and I sailed for South Africa immediately. Although I was no longer in the army, I had to be at the heart of the fighting to make sure that my reports were accurate. I was captured and kept as a prisoner of war. After a month, I managed to escape and walked for about 483 kilometres to safety, but, instead of returning to England, I rejoined the army. This time I was an officer in the South African Light Horse regiment. The British won the war and although we celebrated our victory, over 3,000 of our soldiers had died and more than 10,600 men had been treated at the hospital. When I returned to the UK, I wrote the book *London to Ladysmith via Pretoria*.

◆ ◆ ◆

In 1900, there was another election and this time I was elected as the Member of Parliament (MP) for Oldham. Before I began my new career, I went on a speaking tour. My books and the stories I had written as a wartime journalist had created quite a lot of interest and people wanted to hear me talking about my experiences. I went all around the UK and then to the USA and Canada, and I was paid more than £5,000.

Being an MP was just like being in a war, but using words to fight battles instead of weapons. I no longer believed in the <u>principles</u> of the Conservative Party and in 1904, I joined the <u>Liberal</u> Party. A year later, I became a Minister for the <u>Colonies</u> and then three years after that, I was promoted to President of the Board of Trade.

In the same year, 1908, I married Clementine Hozier. I first met her in 1904 and again by chance at a dinner party in March 1908. It was an unexpected meeting that changed my life for the better. On 11th August we got engaged and then got married just a month after, on 12th September. During the next 12 years, we had five children but in 1921, our fourth child, called Marigold, died of an infection when she was 2 years old. In a normal week, there was little opportunity for me to be with the family. While Clementine focused on the children, I focused on the country.

In 1910, at just 36 years of age, I became Home Secretary. This is the person in charge of the police force and deciding who has the right to enter the country. It was a difficult time for the UK and I was under a great deal of pressure. In Wales, miners were striking over a disagreement with the owners of the mine and in London there were women, called suffragettes, who were campaigning for the right to vote. Many people, men and women, had started protesting in the streets and there was violence. I had to make some difficult decisions that resulted in both miners and suffragettes being arrested. My actions did not make me popular with the people of Britain and in fact, my decision to send soldiers to Wales to keep the peace made me unpopular with the Welsh for my entire life. I also tried to find a solution to the 'suffragette problem' by suggesting that a referendum was held. This would be a national vote to decide if women should also have the right to vote. My suggestion was not taken seriously and I was unpopular, too, with my colleagues for having made it in the first place.

In 1911, I became First <u>Lord</u> of the Admiralty, making me in charge of the Royal Navy. I thought it was funny that I should be in command of the navy when I was really an army man. When I discovered aeroplanes, or 'flying machines' as they were first called, my passion for them could only be matched by the passion I previously had for horses. In my view, aeroplanes were going to be at the heart of all future battles and to emphasize their importance, I took flying lessons.

We needed to strengthen the navy and I ordered newer and larger <u>warships</u> to be built. Many MPs and military people objected to the cost of this development and wanted to continue using horses in war, but I believed that the days of the cavalry were over. I also thought it was necessary for us to have more <u>tanks</u> and to start using aeroplanes. I spoke loudly and often about the subject but my comments were not welcome as it was generally thought that I should limit my opinions to the navy and not interfere in other departments.

In 1914, the First World War started as Germany attacked its neighbours. The conflict soon involved the nations of the

British Empire and fighting in Europe expanded to Turkey. I planned a naval attack in Gallipoli in Turkey, which was not successful and as a result, it was necessary to bring in soldiers from Australia and New Zealand. We were defeated and it was reported that over half a million men were killed or injured. I was blamed for the whole disaster, which did not help to improve my popularity, and as a punishment, I was <u>demoted</u> and given a much less important position in the government. I resigned and joined the army.

On 22nd November 1916, at the age of 42, I reported for duty in the battlefields in France. I was <u>commander</u> of a large group of soldiers who fought bravely. Conditions were terrible and with my soldiers, I slept, ate and fought in thick mud that stuck to everything. On returning to Britain, in 1917, I spoke in Parliament about finding a way to end the war, and having had experience in the battlefields, I was made minister of Munitions – which were military supplies such as weapons. To everyone's relief, in November 1918, the nations involved in the war decided to end the fighting.

◆ ◆ ◆

In 1919, I was made Secretary of State for War. A revolution in Russia had taken place, giving the <u>Communists</u> power and although I was concerned, we had our own problems to deal with at home. In 1921, I was made Secretary of State for the Colonies. I signed the Anglo-Irish Treaty which brought an end to the Irish War of Independence. Two governments were made. The first was in Belfast in Northern Ireland, which had been created the previous year and controlled six counties in the north east. The other was in Dublin and had authority over the rest of Ireland. Eire – Southern Ireland – became a self-governing state within the British Empire, and Northern Ireland remained under British rule.

For the next two years I was not involved professionally with politics. I lost my <u>seat</u> in the next general election but in 1924, I became an MP again, this time back with the Conservatives. I was Chancellor of the Exchequer, which meant that I was in charge of taxes and <u>public spending</u>. I made the decision that Britain would return to the Gold Standard – that the value of British currency would be connected to the value of gold – and as a result, our prices in world markets were not competitive. My decision created major social problems, and serious unemployment resulted in the General Strike of 1926. Thousands of people, led by the miners, arrived in London to demonstrate, and in fear of <u>civil war</u>, the police had to keep order, often by force. It was a difficult time and worse was to follow when in 1929, the <u>stock markets</u> in London and New York crashed. Companies were ruined, businesses closed and people were without work once again. In the elections in 1929, the Conservatives lost and although I was still an MP, I no longer had a position in the government.

I spent my time at home writing books. One was called *A History of the English-Speaking Peoples*. I was doing less public speaking and when I did, few people listened. We were facing problems in India, because of Gandhi's campaign for the British to leave and to allow India to rule itself. Also, I had a strong feeling that in Germany, the National Socialist Party which had come to power in the country's national

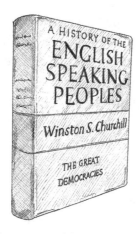

elections would bring trouble to Europe and particularly to Britain. In my book, *The Gathering Storm*, I advised that Britain should invest more money in the military forces as I was sure there was going to be another war. The economy of the country was struggling for survival and I was ignored. I continued writing and painting as both of these activities gave me a chance to be by myself and do things my way. It was most satisfying, but, surprisingly, my life was about to change.

◆ ◆ ◆

As Hitler sent his German army into Poland, Britain declared war on Germany on 3rd September 1939. The Prime Minister, Neville Chamberlain, made me First Lord of the Admiralty and once again I was in charge of a war campaign. However, it was clear that our island was not ready for battle. Chamberlain resigned and, in 1940, I was asked by King George VI to replace him. Many people wanted me to continue Chamberlain's efforts to try to get peace with Germany but I refused, telling the nation in a speech that became famous that we would fight and that it would require "blood, toil, tears and sweat".

In 1940, the Battle of Britain began and five years of war followed. In the beginning, Britain stood alone, as European countries were invaded. In 71 air attacks, German planes dropped bombs in Britain's biggest cities, destroying many homes and killing many civilians. I had always believed that using aeroplanes in battle was the most useful weapon and I was proved right. The heroic acts of the Royal Air Force in the Battle of Britain saved us from being defeated by the Germans. The USA kept out of the war until it was attacked by the Japanese, and Russia joined the fight after being invaded by the Germans.

I made decisions during the war that both saved lives and caused deaths and, for a long time, nobody knew who was going to win. To win, we had to free France, which had been invaded and occupied by the German army, and invade Germany. We also had to fight in Africa and in Italy. In 1942, I had meetings with President Roosevelt of the USA and Joseph Stalin, who was the leader of the Soviet Union, as there had to be a partnership with the Russians and the Americans. They persuaded me that it was vital for us to attack German forces in France, on land and in the air. In April 1944, General Eisenhower, General Montgomery, King George VI and myself watched a rehearsal of the planned attack that was then called D-Day. On 6th June 1944, D-Day arrived and our soldiers crossed the sea to Normandy in France. Fierce fighting throughout the country followed, ending nine months later, when

Germany gave their <u>unconditional surrender</u>. On 8th May 1945 people were dancing and singing in the streets of Britain as VE Day – Victory in Europe – was celebrated.

In the General Election in 1945, I expected the Conservative Party to win but to my surprise, we lost. It was as if the people thought that the man who had led them in war was not the right person to lead them in peace. Once again I returned to writing and painting and two years later when I learned I had won a Nobel Prize for Literature, I was really quite shocked. I was elected as Prime Minister again in 1951, but in 1955, I resigned as I was experiencing health problems. I stayed active in politics until I was 89 years old and on 24th January 1965, aged 90, I died at home. Queen Elizabeth II wanted me to have one final honour and I was given a magnificent state funeral at St Paul's Cathedral in London.

The Life of Winston Churchill

1874 — Winston Leonard Spencer-Churchill was born on 30th November, in Oxfordshire, England. He was the son of a leading Conservative politician, Lord Randolph Churchill. His mother was the daughter of American millionaire Leonard Jerome.

1876–1880 — Between the ages of 2 and 6, Winston lived in Dublin, Ireland. He formed a close bond with his nanny, Elizabeth Ann Everest.

1882–1888 — He went to two different primary schools.

1888–1893 — Winston enrolled at Harrow School.

1893 — He attended the Royal Military Academy, Sandhurst. A year later, he graduated.

1895 — Winston joined the 4th Hussars. While on holiday, he travelled to Cuba and sent reports on a conflict for the *Daily Graphic* newspaper.

1896 — He was sent to Bombay, India, as a cavalry officer.

1897 — Winston fought with the Malakand Field Force against local soldiers. He sent reports to British newspapers, and then published his first book, *The Story of the Malakand Field Force*.

1898   Winston was part of the expeditionary force that was sent to Egypt, to reclaim Sudan as a British territory.

1899   He resigned from the army, went to the Boer War as a journalist and was captured. After escaping, he joined the South African Light Horse army.

1900   Winston returned to England. He was elected as a Conservative MP for Oldham. He wrote the book *London to Ladysmith via Pretoria*.

1904–1905   Winston left the Conservatives and joined the Liberals and became Under Secretary of State for the Colonies.

1906   Winston published *Lord Randolph Churchill*, a biography of his father. He was elected as the Member of Parliament (MP) for Oldham in the general election.

1908   Churchill became MP for Dundee, Scotland in local elections. He married Clementine Hozier, and they had five children.

1910–1911   He became Home Secretary and then First Lord of the Admiralty.

1914   The First World War began. A year later,
        Winston was demoted, after his planned
        attack of the Dardenelles and Gallipoli left
        thousands dead.

1916   Winston resigned from the government
        and rejoined the Army. He became a
        Lieutenant-Colonel.

1917   He became Minister for Munitions.

1919   Winston was appointed Secretary of State
        for War and Secretary for Air until 1921.

1921   He became Secretary of State for the
        Colonies. He signed the Anglo-Irish
        Treaty, which established the Irish Free
        State. His daughter, Marigold, died.

1922   Winston lost his seat as MP for Dundee in
        Scotland in the general election.

1924   Once re-elected to Parliament, Winston
        was made Chancellor of the Exchequer. He
        supervised the return of the Gold Standard.
        He also rejoined the Conservative Party.

1930s   Winston wrote *Marlborough: His Life and
        Times* and *A History of the English-Speaking
        Peoples*.

1939   He signed the British–Russian anti-
        Nazi agreement. Britain declared war on
        Germany. Winston was appointed First
        Lord of the Admiralty.

1940   Winston was made Prime Minister at
        the request of the King, after Neville
        Chamberlain resigned.

1941   The Atlantic Charter was signed by
        Franklin Roosevelt and Winston Churchill.

1942   Winston met with USSR leader Joseph
        Stalin and US President Roosevelt. He
        approved the policy of heavy bombing of
        German cities.

1944   He met with Franklin Roosevelt at the
        second Quebec Conference. He discussed
        the D-Day plan with General Eisenhower,
        General Montgomery, and King George
        VI. A two-day war conference was held in
        Marrakesh, with General de Gaulle of France.

1945   The Second World War ended in Europe.
        Winston signed The Yalta Agreement with
        Roosevelt and Stalin. They decided on how
        Europe should be divided. He resigned as
        Prime Minister after his government was
        defeated in the general election.

1951   Winston was elected Prime Minister for a
        second term.

1953   He won a Nobel Prize for Literature.

1955   Winston resigned as Prime Minister.

1964   He left the government and spent most of
       his time at Chartwell, his country home in
       Kent, England.

1965   Winston Churchill died aged 90, in
       London. His funeral at St Paul's Cathedral
       was one of history's largest state funerals.

Che Guevara

◆ ◆ ◆

1928–1967

the Argentinian doctor who fought for revolution

When I was a young man, I saw poor people everywhere who did not have the power to change their lives. I couldn't help everyone, but I did help the people of Cuba. I became a revolutionary and fought for their right for a better life.

◆ ◆ ◆

I was born on 14th June 1928 in a large city in Argentina called Rosario and my parents named me Ernesto, like my father. I had two brothers and two sisters, all younger than me and we had a happy, <u>privileged</u> childhood. My father's family were from an Irish background and my mother's had originally been from Spain. My father was a civil engineer – a person who plans, designs and builds roads, bridges, harbours and public buildings. My mother's name was Celia and she was busy looking after all of us.

In 1933, when I was 4 years old, we moved to a place called Alta Gracia, also in Argentina. My parents taught me at home for four years until I started going to the local primary school. My father also taught me how to play chess and I liked reading poetry. I loved all kinds of sport but I suffered quite badly from asthma – a condition of the lungs that makes breathing difficult – and when I was only 2 years old, I nearly died in a particularly bad asthma attack. Although I was asthmatic all my life, I loved sport and didn't let my breathing problems stop me from playing rugby, football and golf. I enjoyed swimming, too, but most of all, I loved cycling.

Because I was often unwell, I spent a lot of time at home and my parents encouraged me to read as much as I could. Despite our middle-class lifestyle, both of my parents had left-wing beliefs. From a young age, I had strong beliefs, too, and I was interested in philosophy. In primary school, I was fascinated by the Spanish Civil War, which was coming to an end, and I wanted to know what was going to happen to the refugees from the war. In 1943, we moved to Córdoba and I started my second year of high school. One of my best friends at school, Tita, was a member of the Argentine Communist Youth and we discussed the works of Karl Marx and other left-wing writers and philosophers. In particular, I thought about the many people living near us who were in a state of extreme poverty and I wondered what I could do to help them. I decided to become a doctor and I worked hard at school, graduating in 1946. The next year, when my family moved to Buenos Aires, the capital of Argentina, I went with them and in 1948, I enrolled at the Medical School of the University of Buenos Aires.

In 1950, when I was 22 years old, I wanted to discover more about my country and how people lived and so I set out on a 4,500-kilometre journey to northern Argentina by bicycle. I had put a small motor on my bicycle but even so, progress was slow. One of the places I visited, called San Francisco del Chañar, was near Córdoba. A friend of mine from Córdoba, Alberto Granado, was working at the pharmacy of the leper centre in San Francisco del Chañar, and I wanted to see him. Leprosy was a terrible disease that damaged people's flesh and often made them look awful. People suffering from the disease – lepers – were usually sent to special centres away from the general population, as it was believed that leprosy was easily spread from person to person.

People without specific medical knowledge were often afraid and usually <u>disgusted</u> by the disease and the people suffering from it. I was not, and when I arrived at the centre, I started talking to patients, and I became more interested in every aspect of the disease.

Before I set out on my trip, I decided to keep a diary and to write down everything that I saw and heard. I enjoyed taking notes, and writing in the diary became a habit that I continued on later trips. Later, my family turned my notes into a book and in 1993, *The Motorcycle Diaries* was published.

◆ ◆ ◆

In 1951, I took a year off from my studies and spent six months working as a nurse on a huge ship, belonging to the Argentine National Shipping Company, that transported petrol. The ship stopped in various places in Brazil,

Venezuela and the island of Trinidad in the Caribbean, before heading back to Argentina. Then, with my friend, Alberto, I set off on a motorcycle tour of South America, visiting Ecuador, Colombia, Venezuela, Panama and Peru. On this trip, Alberto started calling me Che, because in spoken Spanish *che* means 'friend' or 'man' and apparently I used it all the time when I was speaking. The name stuck and I was never called Ernesto again.

In Peru, I spent time working at the San Pablo Leper Colony and I was shocked by the conditions inside the colony and by the way the patients were treated. I was also shocked at the living conditions of the poor who did not have leprosy. In village after village and town after town, I saw severe poverty, with the poor unable to live in decent housing or to have enough food. There were few medical facilities and disease was everywhere. Death rates among the poor were high but all around I could see wealth. There was wealth in the fields, in the mines and factories, so why were so many people poor?

I came to the conclusion that poor people were being exploited by the rich. There was no other explanation. I knew that this situation had to change, or be changed by people like myself. I decided that when I qualified as a doctor, I would not look after patients who could afford the best doctors. I would look after those who would never have the money for even the most basic medical care. It was not my only dream. As we travelled from one country to the next, I had another vision and that was for all the states in South America to become united.

◆ ◆ ◆

In 1953, I got my medical degree and I qualified to be a doctor. If I hadn't had asthma, I would have had to do military service but I was free and I set off to find people I could help. I soon discovered that it was not going to be as easy as I had previously thought. My knowledge and skills were not enough. I needed to do more than say what was wrong with patients and give them advice. I needed drugs and <u>surgical</u> equipment and that cost money, which was not available, so I became angry and disappointed. I went to many places, some of which I had visited during my previous trip: Bolivia, Peru, Ecuador, Panama, Nicaragua, Costa Rica, Honduras, El Salvador, finally going to Guatemala, where I stayed for a while.

In Costa Rica, it had been clear where all the money was. In 1882, the Costa Rican government had gone into business with an American businessman called Keith, building the national railroad. The government had been unable to pay its share of the costs and was in debt to the American. As part payment, the government gave Keith 3,200 square kilometres of land so that he could grow bananas to send back to the USA and The United Fruit Company was created. Bananas were very popular in North America and the company, which had a <u>monopoly</u> in Central and South America, was making huge profits. However, I saw that the money that was made in Costa Rica went back to the USA and was not used to pay local workers properly or give them decent living conditions. This made me furious and I called the company 'Capitalist <u>octopuses</u>', promising myself that I would not rest until I saw their destruction. For the first time, I considered that perhaps medicine was not the answer to the problems of poverty after all. Maybe soldiers and weapons were needed to physically fight against those in power.

In Guatemala, however, it seemed that the government was more in control. The president, Jacobo Arbenz, reclaimed all uncultivated land – land where no crops were being grown – and gave it to local people so that they could start their own farms. The United Fruit Company was greatly affected by this as they had lost 910 square kilometres of their land. United Fruit had considerable influence within the American government. For example, one of the shareholders was the US Secretary of State. The US government viewed Arbenz as being pro-communist and a threat to democracy – at that time their anti-communist campaign was intense. They overlooked the fact that Arbenz had been elected in democratic elections, however, and a coup was planned to remove him from power. It lasted eight days and although Arbenz's army tried to fight back, his resignation was announced on 26th June 1954. Almost all of the people in Arbenz's government were forced to leave the country in fear of their lives. I had fought and spoken out against the coup and as a result, my life, too, was in danger. I managed to escape and went to live in Mexico City, where I worked at the General Hospital.

◆ ◆ ◆

In Guatemala, I had met a woman from Peru called Hilda Gadea Acosta, an economist and protest leader who was, like me, determined to help the poor. She had come with me to Mexico City and in September 1955 we got married. The following year Hilda gave birth to our daughter, Hildita – little Hilda. Unfortunately our feelings for each other did not last and after four years our marriage ended.

The USA's military coup in Guatemala had convinced me that it was necessary to fight for the rights of the poor, who had neither a voice nor a direction. I could provide both of these and I became a revolutionary. I needed to earn a living, so I gave some lectures on medicine and I tried to use my skills as a doctor to help those in need, but my thoughts were more on politics. One day, I met Raul Castro, who introduced me to his brother, Fidel.

Fidel Castro, a Cuban living in Mexico, was concerned about the social injustice in Cuba. As in many other places in the world, a small percentage of the population had all the power. These were the owners of the Haciendas – the large farms that grew crops like sugar and tobacco – and they were rich. The rest of the people worked on the farms. There were laws that stated how much produce each hacienda could grow in a year and this meant that there were often long periods of time when crops were not being grown. This was not a problem for the owners, who had more than enough money to live well until the next crop was harvested and sold. However, for the workers, who did not have money or property, this meant unemployment and suffering. Nearly half of them were illiterate. More than 65 per cent lived without running water and only 1 in 14 families had electricity. They lived in huts with earth floors and only four per cent ate meat regularly. They had almost no access to education or medical facilities. Even though

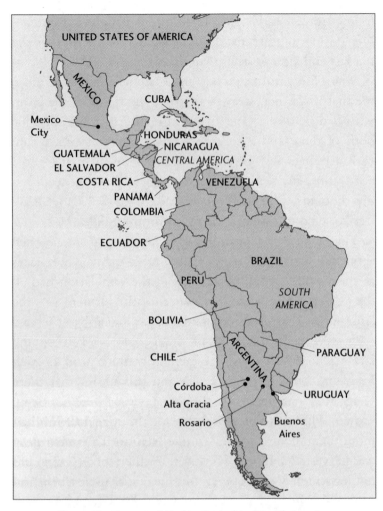

Places Che Guevara visited in Central and South America

there were five times as many workers as hacienda-owners, there was no way the workers could change the situation.

In 1952, Castro tried to win a <u>seat</u> in the government in the elections, which would give him the power to make changes in society. It was generally believed that his party, Ortodoxo, would win, but before the elections could take place, a general called Batista led a coup, resulting in him becoming a <u>dictator</u>. With the support of the military and the <u>upper classes</u> of Cuban society, Batista's government gained the support of the USA. The following year, Castro and the other members of the Ortodoxo party, approximately 126 people, organized a counter coup – an attempt to reverse the first coup and regain power – which failed. Castro was sentenced to 15 years in prison but in 1955, he was released and went to live in Mexico.

Castro told me that he was planning a revolution to take control of Cuba – the 26th of July Movement he called it – and naturally I wanted to be involved. In the beginning I offered my services as a doctor but I soon became involved in military training. The first stage of our plan was to invade Cuba from an old boat called *The Granma* and on 25th November 1956, we arrived in Cuba. Unfortunately, Batista's army attacked us and many of our soldiers were killed.

Those of us who survived hid in the Sierra Maestra mountains on the southeast coast of Cuba. I was promoted to <u>Commander</u> and for the next two years, we continued to fight. Now that I was second-in-command, I had to be tough with the soldiers. Those who tried to leave without permission and those who turned out to be spies or committed other forms of <u>treason</u>, were shot and people soon began to respect and fear me. On 2nd January 1959, I led our soldiers into the capital, Havana, and we took control from Batista.

Now things were different and it was a time of great excitement in Cuba. Instead of being revolutionaries, we were government ministers and it was time to put our ideals into practice. I introduced new policies, particularly on health and education, providing free health care and schooling for all citizens of Cuba. My goal was for every Cuban to be able to read and write. My personal life was changing, too. I had fallen in love with a woman called Aleida March who had been with us in the mountains. On 2nd June 1959, we got married and over the years, we had four children. However, there was little time for a comfortable home life as we had other work to do.

We had enemies to deal with and especially those that had been Batista's supporters. Some of the changes we were making were unpopular with them and it was decided that those found guilty of war crimes or of being traitors would be executed. We were afraid that if we let them live, they might take justice into their own hands and try to rebel.

One particular change was in the laws that dealt with ownership of land. Firstly, foreigners – non-Cubans – were not allowed to own property. Secondly, it was forbidden for any farm to be larger than four square kilometres. Any land over this limit was given to farm workers or became part of state-owned farms. These were large farms that offered secure employment for the workers. Much of the profit made from selling sugar, tobacco, coffee and beef abroad was spent on building schools, hospitals, and housing.

Very soon after our revolution had taken place, Fidel asked me to travel abroad and talk to other leaders. In 1960, the USA, in revenge for the 1,900 square kilometres of land that American companies had lost, had stopped trading with Cuba and no longer imported goods such as sugar, so we needed international support to survive. On 17th April 1961, a group of 1,400 Cuban <u>exiles</u>, supported by the government of the USA, tried to gain power again in Cuba. They were not successful. The episode was later called the Bay of Pigs Invasion. Our victory strengthened our position and we came to the attention of the Soviet Union. Meanwhile, I published my book, *Guerrilla Warfare*. By this time I had also become Finance Minister, Minister of Industry and the president of the national bank. In 1962, we allowed the Soviet Union to place nuclear <u>missiles</u> in Cuba. Under the very real threat of nuclear war, President Kennedy in the USA persuaded the Soviets to remove the missiles.

♦ ◆ ♦

In 1964, I decided to leave Cuba. I spoke at the United Nations in New York and travelled to Europe, celebrating St Patrick's Day in Ireland – after all, I did have Irish ancestors – and then the following year I moved to Africa. I lived in the Congo, which was a poor country that was rich in valuable minerals, such as gold, copper and diamonds. Once again I saw local people being exploited and I wondered if revolutionary action would be successful. Local leadership was not well organized and after seven months we stopped fighting. My efforts had failed and I was fortunate to escape.

I went to Bolivia in 1966 and I tried to start another revolution there, changing my name to Adolfo Mena Gonzalez. The Bolivians working in the mines and fields had long been exploited but, to my surprise, they were not willing to fight for their rights. I had a small army of fighters but the Bolivian Government's army was supported by the USA and after 11 months, I was caught. On 9th October 1967, when I was 39 years old, I was executed with my men.

'Was it all worth it?' you may ask. Could I have done more by being a doctor and not a fighter? Perhaps, but I felt that the poor deserved a better life and that I had to fight to help them get it. I died fighting for my beliefs and that was good enough for me.

The Life of Che Guevara

1928   Che was born on 14th June in Rosario, Argentina. His parents named him Ernesto. He was the eldest of five children.

1930   He had his first asthma attack.

1933   Che and family moved to Alta Gracia in Argentina. A year later, his parents began to teach him at home.

1937   He enrolled in primary school.

1942   Che began high school at *Colegio Nacional Dean Funes*. The following year, his family moved to Córdoba.

1946   He graduated from high school.

1947–1948   Che moved to Buenos Aires with his family, and entered the University of Buenos Aires to study medicine.

1950   He went on a solo expedition to Northern Argentina. Che travelled by bicycle equipped with a small motor. Along the way, he kept a diary of his travels.

1951   Che took a year off his studies, and worked as a nurse for six months on a ship carrying petrol. He then went on a motorcycle trip through South America with his friend, Alberto Granando. He became known as "Che".

1952   Che and Alberto continued on their trip with the intention of becoming volunteers at a leper colony in San Pablo. The trip took them through Argentina, Chile, Peru, Ecuador, Colombia, Venezuela, Panama, and Florida, USA, before returning to Buenos Aires. Che had a vision of all the states in South America becoming united.

1953   Che graduated from university with a Degree in Medicine. He set out again to Bolivia, Peru, Ecuador, Panama, Costa Rica, Nicaragua, Honduras and El Salvador. His trip ended in Guatemala, where he stayed.

1954   President Arbenz of Guatemala was forced to resign after a coup resulted in his government losing power. Che went to Mexico and worked in the General Hospital. He gave lectures on medicine at the Autonomous University of Mexico.

1955   Che married Hilda Gadea, who was politically connected to the American Popular Revolutionary Alliance. Four years later their marriage ended. During that time, he met Fidel Castro and joined the revolutionary movement.

1956   He sailed on *The Granma* in an attack on Cuba as the first stage in the revolutionary plan known as the 26th of July Movement. Che and Hilda had a daughter.

1957   Che became a revolutionary fighter in the
       Sierra Maestra mountains. He was promoted
       to Commandant.

1958   Under Che's command, the city of Santa
       Clara was captured.

1959   The Batista dictatorship in Cuba was
       overthrown. Che married Aleida March.
       Fidel Castro gained more political power in
       Cuba. Che became President of the National
       Bank of Cuba.

1960   Ernesto and Aleida had their first child. They
       later had three more children. The USA
       reacted to the Revolutionary Movement by
       reducing the import of Cuban sugar.

1961   Che became Minister of Industries. He began
       education changes in Cuba, specifically
       focussing on reading and writing. The
       US-trained Cuban exiles invaded Cuba in the
       Bay of Pigs Invasion. Che published his book
       Guerrilla Warfare.

1962   Che developed a Soviet-Cuban relationship,
       leading to the Cuban Missile Crisis. The
       following year, he published the book,
       Episodes of the Cuban Revolutionary War.

1964   He decided to leave Cuba. As head of the
       Cuban representatives, Che spoke to the
       United Nations, and travelled to Africa to
       fight the revolutionary cause abroad.

1965   Che wrote a farewell letter to Fidel Castro.
       He travelled to the Congo to continue the
       revolution. It was judged to be a failure after
       seven months.

1966   Che lived in Dar Es Salaam, Prague, Cuba,
       and then Bolivia. He wrote his life story.

1967   Che was captured in Quebrada del Yuro.
       He was executed aged 39, in La Higuera,
       Vallegrande, Bolivia.

◆ Glossary ◆

advisor COUNTABLE NOUN
An **advisor** is someone whose job
is to advise important or powerful
people on a particular subject.

Anglican ADJECTIVE
Anglican means belonging or
relating to the Church of England,
or to the churches related to it.

appeal COUNTABLE NOUN
An **appeal** is a request to a court
to change the decision of an
earlier trial.

aristocracy COUNTABLE NOUN
The **aristocracy** is a class of
people in some countries who
have a high social rank and
special titles.

aristocratic ADJECTIVE
Aristocratic means belonging to
or typical of the aristocracy.

Asia Minor PROPER NOUN
Asia Minor is the old name for
the most western part of Asia. It
is now called Anatolia and is in
modern Turkey.

astronomy UNCOUNTABLE NOUN
Astronomy is the scientific
study of the stars, planets, and
other natural objects in space.

Battle of Britain PROPER NOUN
The Battle of Britain was a
battle fought in the air over the
south-east of England in 1940
between planes of the British
and German air forces.

BCE
You use **BCE** in dates to indicate
a number of years or centuries
before the year in which Jesus
Christ is believed to have been
born. It is an abbreviation for
'before common era'.

behead VERB
If someone **is beheaded**, they
are killed by having their head
cut off, usually as punishment for
a serious crime.

betray TRANSITIVE VERB
If you **betray** someone who
trusts you, you deliberately do
something which hurts them and
causes them harm.

boarding school VARIABLE NOUN
A **boarding school** is a school
where the pupils live during the
term.

chariot COUNTABLE NOUN
In ancient times, **chariots** were
fast-moving vehicles with two
wheels that were pulled by horses.

civil rights PLURAL NOUN
Civil rights are the rights that people have to equal treatment and equal opportunities, whatever their race, sex, or religion.

civil war COUNTABLE NOUN
A **civil war** is a war which is fought between different groups of people living in the same country.

colonist COUNTABLE NOUN
Colonists are people who live in a colony, especially Europeans who went to live in North and South America in the 17th and 18th centuries.

colony COUNTABLE NOUN
1 A **colony** is a country that does not govern itself, but is governed by another, more powerful country.

2 A **colony** is a group of people of a particular sort who live together away from other people.

commander COUNTABLE NOUN
A **commander** is an important military officer in charge of a large group of soldiers or of a whole army.

communist COUNTABLE NOUN
A **communist** is someone who supports a political system in which the state owns and controls all property and all means of production, and everyone is supposed to be equal.

conquer TRANSITIVE VERB
If one country or army **conquers** another country, they take complete control of it.

Conservative Party
PROPER NOUN
The Conservative Party is the main right-of-centre party in Britain.

constitution COUNTABLE NOUN
The **constitution** of a country is the system of laws which formally state people's rights and duties.

coronation COUNTABLE NOUN
A **coronation** is a ceremony at which a crown is put on the head of someone so that they officially become a king or queen.

coup COUNTABLE NOUN
When there is a **coup**, a group of people get rid of the government and take control of a country, sometimes by force.

court
royal court COUNTABLE NOUN
The **court** of a king or queen is the place where he or she lives and works.

crown TRANSITIVE VERB
When a king or queen **is crowned**, a crown is placed on their head as part of a ceremony in which they are officially made king or queen.

delegate COUNTABLE NOUN
A **delegate** is a person who has been sent to vote or make decisions on behalf of a group of people, especially at a conference or meeting.

demote TRANSITIVE VERB
If someone **is demoted**, they are moved to a less important rank or job, often as a punishment for having done something wrong or badly.

dictator COUNTABLE NOUN
A **dictator** is a ruler who has complete power in a country.

disgust TRANSITIVE VERB
If you **are disgusted** by something, it makes you feel a strong sense of dislike and disapproval.

empire COUNTABLE NOUN
An **empire** is a group of countries controlled by one powerful country.

execute TRANSITIVE VERB
When someone **is executed**, they are officially killed as a punishment.

execution UNCOUNTABLE NOUN
Execution is the official killing of someone as a punishment for a serious crime.

exile COUNTABLE NOUN
An **exile** is someone who lives in a foreign country for political reasons.

fleet COUNTABLE NOUN
A **fleet** is an organized group of ships.

governess COUNTABLE NOUN
A **governess** is a woman who is employed by a family to live with them and educate their children.

heir COUNTABLE NOUN
Someone's **heir** is the person who will get their money, property, or title when they die.

house COUNTABLE NOUN
1 **House** can be used to refer to the name of a royal family. For example, in Britain the royal family is the House of Windsor.

2 A **house** is a parliament or other governing group of people.

house arrest UNCOUNTABLE NOUN
If someone is **under house arrest**, they are officially ordered not to leave their home.

humiliation UNCOUNTABLE NOUN
Humiliation is the embarrassment and shame you feel when someone makes you appear stupid, or when you make a mistake in public.

illiterate ADJECTIVE
Someone who is **illiterate** cannot read or write.

imprison TRANSITIVE VERB
If someone **is imprisoned**, they are kept in prison for a period of time.

influential ADJECTIVE
Someone who is **influential** has the power to influence and control other people or events.

inherit TRANSITIVE VERB
If you **inherit** money or property, you receive it from someone who has died.

injustice UNCOUNTABLE NOUN
Injustice is great unfairness in a situation.

intense ADJECTIVE
Something that is **intense** is very extreme in strength or degree.

interpretation VARIABLE NOUN
An **interpretation** of something is an opinion or explanation of what it means.

knight TRANSITIVE VERB
If a man **is knighted**, he is officially given a high rank by the king or queen and can use the title 'sir'.

Labour PROPER NOUN
Labour or **the Labour Party** is the main left-of-centre political party in Britain.

left-wing ADJECTIVE
Left-wing political beliefs and ideas are based on socialism.

legacy COUNTABLE NOUN
A leader's **legacy** is his or her achievements or failures that continue to be significant after he or she dies or stops being a leader.

liberal COUNTABLE NOUN
In Britain, the **Liberals** were members of the Liberal Party. **Liberals** believed in limited controls on industry, the providing of welfare services, and more local government and individual freedom.

lisp COUNTABLE NOUN
If someone has **a lisp**, they pronounce the sounds 's' and 'z' as if they were 'th'. For example, they say 'thing' instead of 'sing'.

lord COUNTABLE NOUN
In Britain, a **lord** is a man who has a high rank in the nobility.

luxurious ADJECTIVE
Something that is **luxurious** is very comfortable and expensive.

middle class COUNTABLE NOUN
The middle class or **middle classes** are the people in a society who are not working class or upper class, for example managers, doctors, and lawyers.
ADJECTIVE
Middle-class people and families belong to the middle classes.

missile COUNTABLE NOUN
A **missile** is a tube-shaped weapon that moves long distances through the air and explodes when it reaches its target.

monarchy VARIABLE NOUN
A **monarchy** is a country in which a king or queen is the head of state. In an **absolute monarchy**, the king or queen has all the power and does not need to listen to elected politicians.

monopoly VARIABLE NOUN
If a company, person, or state has a **monopoly on** something such as an industry, they have complete control over it, and no other company, person, or state can be involved.

nanny COUNTABLE NOUN
A **nanny** is a person who is paid by parents to look after their children.

negotiate TRANSITIVE VERB, INTRANSITIVE VERB
If you **negotiate with** someone, you talk to them in order to reach an agreement about something such as a business deal or a political problem.

negotiation UNCOUNTABLE NOUN
Negotiation is the activity of talking to someone in order to reach an agreement about something such as a business deal or a political problem.

occupy TRANSITIVE VERB
If soldiers **have occupied** a country, they have moved into it and used force in order to gain control of it.

octopus VARIABLE NOUN
An **octopus** is a sea creature with a round body and eight long arms.

officially ADVERB
If something happens **officially**, it is approved by the government or by someone else in authority.

opposition UNCOUNTABLE NOUN
Opposition is strong disagreement with a person, belief, or situation, often involving attempts to stop something happening or continuing.

pardon COUNTABLE NOUN
If someone is given a **pardon**, the authorities say that they will not punish them for something wrong that they have done.

pearl COUNTABLE NOUN
A **pearl** is a hard, shiny, white ball-shaped object which grows inside the shell of an oyster. Pearls are used for making valuable jewellery.

plantation COUNTABLE NOUN
A **plantation** is a large area of land where crops such as cotton, tea, or sugar are grown.

postal ADJECTIVE
A **postal** service or system is the organization and operation of the public service of carrying letters and packages from one place to another.

principle COUNTABLE NOUN
The **principles** of a political party are the basic beliefs it has about the way people should behave and organize themselves.

privileged ADJECTIVE
Someone who is **privileged** has an advantage or opportunity that most other people do not have, usually because of their wealth or high social class.

Protestant COUNTABLE NOUN
A **Protestant** is someone who belongs to the branch of the Christian church which separated from the Catholic church in the sixteenth century.

Prussia PROPER NOUN
Prussia was a powerful German state in northern and central Germany. It became a kingdom in 1701, and was involved in many European wars.

public spending
UNCOUNTABLE NOUN
Public spending is all the money that the government of a country spends on things like the army, roads, education etc.

pursuit SINGULAR NOUN
Your **pursuit of** something that you want consists of your attempts at achieving it.

ransom VARIABLE NOUN
A **ransom** is money that is demanded as payment for the return of someone who has been kidnapped.

rebellion VARIABLE NOUN
A **rebellion** is a violent organized action by a large group of people who are trying to get rid of their country's rulers and change the political system.

regiment COUNTABLE NOUN
In the British army, a **regiment** is a large group of soldiers commanded by a colonel.

resignation VARIABLE NOUN
Someone's **resignation** is the formal statement that they intend to leave their job or position.

rightful ADJECTIVE
Someone's **rightful** place or position is the one that they should have because the law or an authority says that they should have it.

royalty UNCOUNTABLE NOUN
The members of a royal family can be referred to as **royalty**.

ruling COUNTABLE NOUN
A **ruling** is an official decision about a matter, given by someone in authority.

sanitation UNCOUNTABLE NOUN
Sanitation is the process of keeping places clean and hygienic, especially by providing clean water for drinking and cooking, and by taking away dirty water.

seat COUNTABLE NOUN
A **seat** is an official position as a member of an elected parliament.

serve TRANSITIVE VERB
To **serve** your country, an organization, or a person means to do useful work for them because you think it is your duty.

settler COUNTABLE NOUN
Settlers are people who go to live in a new country.

shareholder COUNTABLE NOUN
A **shareholder** is someone who owns one or more of the equal parts that a company is divided into. **Shareholders** can vote on how the company is run, and usually get a share of the profits every year.

slavery UNCOUNTABLE NOUN
Slavery is the system by which people are owned by other people as slaves.

spill (spills, spilling, spilled or **spilt)** TRANSITIVE VERB
If you say that blood **has been spilt**, you mean there has been a lot of violence and fighting, and people have been killed and badly hurt.

stand (stands, standing or **stood)**
to stand in someone's way
PHRASE
If you **stand in** someone's **way**, you try to stop them doing what they are trying to do.

stock market COUNTABLE NOUN
The stock market consists of the activity of buying stocks and shares, and the people and institutions that organize it.

stutter COUNTABLE NOUN
If someone has a **stutter**, they have difficulty speaking because they keep repeating the first sound of a word.

superior COUNTABLE NOUN
Your **superiors** in an organization are the people who have a higher rank than you.

surgical ADJECTIVE
Surgical equipment is the equipment that a doctor needs in order to treat people by cutting them open so that he or she can repair, remove, or replace a diseased or damaged part.

surrender INTRANSITIVE VERB
If an army or country **surrenders**, they stop fighting a battle or war and agree that they have been beaten.
UNCOUNTABLE NOUN
Surrender is the act of officially admitting you have lost a battle or war.
Unconditional surrender is when you admit defeat and do not ask for anything in exchange.

tank COUNTABLE NOUN
A **tank** is a powerful military vehicle covered with strong metal and equipped with guns or rockets.

throne SINGULAR NOUN
You can talk about **the throne** to refer to the position of being king, queen, or emperor.

tobacco VARIABLE NOUN
Tobacco is a plant that grows in hot areas. Its dried leaves are used to make cigarettes and cigars.

toil UNCOUNTABLE NOUN
If you describe work as **toil**, you mean that it is hard work that involves doing very unpleasant or tiring tasks.

Tower of London PROPER NOUN
The **Tower of London** is a castle in London. It was a royal palace and also served as a prison for important or royal prisoners. It is now a museum.

trader COUNTABLE NOUN
Traders are people who buy goods and transport them to sell them somewhere else.

traitor COUNTABLE NOUN
A **traitor** is someone who deliberately does something which helps their country's enemies and which hurts or harms their own country.

treason UNCOUNTABLE NOUN
Treason is the crime of betraying your king or queen or your country.

tribesman COUNTABLE NOUN
Tribesmen are the men who belong to a tribe, which is a group of people of the same race, language, and customs.

upper class COUNTABLE NOUN
The upper class or **the upper classes** are the group of people in a society who own the most property and have the highest social status.

warship COUNTABLE NOUN
A **warship** is a ship with guns that is used for fighting in wars.

will COUNTABLE NOUN
A **will** is a legal document that someone writes, saying what should happen to their money and property after they die.

worship INTRANSITIVE VERB
To **worship** means to show your respect for the God that you believe in, for example by saying prayers.

Collins
English Readers

THE AMAZING PEOPLE READERS SERIES:

Level 1

Amazing Inventors
978-0-00-754494-3

Amazing Leaders
978-0-00-754492-9

Amazing Entrepreneurs and Business People
978-0-00-754501-8

Amazing Women
978-0-00-754493-6

Amazing Performers
978-0-00-754508-7

Level 2

Amazing Aviators
978-0-00-754495-0

Amazing Architects and Artists
978-0-00-754496-7

Amazing Composers
978-0-00-754502-5

Amazing Mathematicians
978-0-00-754503-2

Amazing Medical People
978-0-00-754509-4

Level 3

Amazing Explorers
978-0-00-754497-4

Amazing Writers
978-0-00-754498-1

Amazing Philanthropists
978-0-00-754504-9

Amazing Performers
978-0-00-754505-6

Amazing Scientists
978-0-00-754510-0

Level 4

Amazing Thinkers and Humanitarians
978-0-00-754499-8

Amazing Scientists
978-0-00-754500-1

Amazing Writers
978-0-00-754506-3

Amazing Leaders
978-0-00-754507-0

Amazing Entrepreneurs and Business People
978-0-00-754511-7

Visit **www.collinselt.com/readers** for language activities, teacher's notes, and to find out more about the series.